*America Confronts a Revolutionary World: 1776–1976*

by William Appleman Williams

# AMERICA CONFRONTS A REVOLUTIONARY WORLD: 1776-1976

by
William Appleman Williams

WILLIAM MORROW AND COMPANY, INC.
NEW YORK     1976

Printed in the United States of America.

1  2  3  4  5     80  79  78  77  76

Library of Congress Cataloging in Publication Data

Williams, William Appleman.
  America confronts a revolutionary world, 1776–1976.

  Includes bibliographical references and index.
  1. United States—History—Philosophy. I. Title.
E175.9.W49        973'.01          75-43863
ISBN 0-688-03042-4

BOOK DESIGN: H. ROBERTS

For Wendy Margaret Tomlin

Ain't it good,
Ain't it right,
That you are with me here tonight . . .*

# Contents

# Preface

We Americans are strong on celebrating anniversaries but weak on informing our lives with the history we commemorate. Our sense of the Past—of history in its classical meaning—is weak and limited. When we are not simply nostalgic (which is most of the time), we tend to think of history as an attic to be explored when there is nothing else to do. For that reason, our feel for the Future is cramped and twisted. We see it either as a projection of the Present or as a fantasy to escape unpleasant aspects of the Present.

Those are two of the themes that I will discuss, obliquely as well as directly, in this essay. But I am not offering an abstract discourse, and I make no claim of being unaffected by The Great Vietnam Intervention and The Great Watergate Intervention. Those are inherent elements of the ongoing dialectical encounter between myself and my environment that produced this essay. I became increasingly intrigued, for example, by our inability to see the conflict in Vietnam as a revolutionary war, and by our unwillingness to honor our historical commitment to the revolutionary right to self-determination.

And I found the response to Watergate a fascinating

example of our lack of any significant sense of the Past. For one cannot truly be traumatized by Richard Milhous Nixon and his Hunker-Down-in-the-Bunker Crowd if one knows about Andrew Jackson, Abraham Lincoln, Woodrow Wilson, and Franklin Delano Roosevelt—to name only four other Presidents who were also artisans of evasion and distortion and masters of the craft of accumulating power unto themselves.

In a similar way, a feel for history leaves one largely unimpressed by all the relieved and congratulatory talk about how "the system worked" to control Nixon. For a sense of history in the way that I am using that term illuminates the crucial factor: those other men were also ultimately controlled, *but the process that they personified (and carried forward) has not been controlled.* We citizens of the United States continue to lose ever more of our power to define the issues and the alternatives, and to choose from among those options.

# I

I am intensely aware of the various aspects of that process not only because I am a historian, but also because I live in a nonacademic environment. My neighbors, friends, and acquaintances are longshoremen, loggers, bus and truck drivers, longhairs, independent fishermen, artisans and artists, housewives and liberationists, poor and wealthy, swingers and Bircher-Minutemen, and all of them of all ages.

All but a few of those people cling desperately to a belief in America as an ideal—a truth—that can be realized despite the ever-expanding power of the corporate state we call euphemistically a democratic republic. (The others are out of it.) They all can function as people. Indeed, most of them perform remarkably well within the tiny Fields of the

Lord that yet remain open in this centralized and consolidated bureaucracy. But they cannot break free of the Present because they have no feel of the past to use as a fulcrum for their experience, ideals, and imagination. They are deeply American in the fundamental sense of thinking about America only in terms of the present.

I have the hope that a candid discussion of the way that we Americans have seen our own revolution, and the revolutions that almost immediately began to erupt elsewhere in the world (and which continue to occur), will help us transcend that terribly limited, and restrictive, presentism. In the classical historical sense, we began as, and have remained, a people driven by a profound fear of change. We fear the Past and we fear the Future. We remain serfs in a feudalism of our own creation. We must free ourselves of that slavery if we are to survive—let alone create a humane life together.


# II

To the extent that I am helpful in that endeavor, I am indebted to many other people. Street-corner, barroom, and grocery-store conversations with uncounted citizens have given me more information and ideas than I could list. Undergraduate students have told me so much about America that I have not been able to absorb it all. So have my children. I am deeply and lovingly indebted to them for the seminar they have patiently conducted for my education during these last twenty years.

My more formal debts are easier to define, though no less impossible to repay. Some will be noted in the citations along the way. Others require a special word. Mitzi Mahaffey is one of those. Most of the students in my senior seminar have chosen, over the last seven years, to investigate

America's relationship with one or another twentieth-century revolution. Many of them, such as John Savage and Paul Coon, produced stimulating papers, and the dialogue was generally tough and illuminating.

Mitzi made a particularly important contribution, however, through the combination of her intellectual power and discipline, her perception into relationships, and her experiences in the world of those others—"*They*"—who define our options and concepts. We all learned much from her. At a later date, she uncovered revealing documents and then, in talking about them, helped me make sense of it all.

The encouragement, active help, and criticism offered during this project by the following people require an inclusive acknowledgment: Steve Ambrose, Lloyd Gardner, Walter LaFeber, Gerry McCauley, and Warren Susman. Without them, no book.

My concern with, and emphasis upon, the developing distortion of the American sense of time and history is in one respect inherent in being a historian. Beyond that, however, lie three other considerations. I was first trained as a mathematician and a scientist, and I became fascinated by time *per se*. Then, in the research for this essay, I grew ever more impressed by the way Americans have dismissed the past and conceptualized the future as a projection of the present. Finally, at the end of that work, I reread Loren Baritz's superb book, *City on the Hill. A History of Ideas and Myths in America* (1964), and Warren Susman's mind-bending essay, "The Persistence of American Reform" (1967). Their perceptions into the American sense of time and history reexcited and encouraged me, and I am sure that their insights were silently but effectively tutoring me throughout the intervening years.

The ambience of life in the company of certain people is a magical experience. Ben Murdzek and Bill Mc-Mechan, for example, conduct an ongoing postgraduate seminar in pool and human nature. There is nothing in my experience quite so helpful in maintaining one's perspective as a historian as playing very serious pool with humorous, perceptive, and skillful people. It keeps one's intellect and soul in communion with the interrelatedness—the wholeness—of it all.

Karl Paul Link and Joel Hedgpeth are Renaissance men masquerading as world-renowned scientists. They are wise in ways that must give hope to the Lord. Certainly I have been graced by their friendship and related tutorials.

Over the years, certain friendships that are not primarily intellectual nevertheless sustain and inform one's life and work in ways that transcend any monograph, seminar, or document. These, in particular, are a warm, living part of this essay because they helped me to learn how the present becomes a past that creates a future: Bill and Mick Bonwit, Bud and Frances Burdett, Claydean Cameron, Rob and Barbara Davidson, Marge and Cy Goodwin, Fred and Nancy Harrington, Lew Kreinberg, Elizabeth Link, Orde and Dottie Pinckney, David Shetzline, Charles Vevier, Peter Weiss, and Jeannie Williams.

Thank you all.

Finally, there is the matter of money. The American Philosophical Society, and the American Council of Learned Societies pleaded insufficient funds and graciously declined my requests for assistance. But Hillel Black arranged a helpful advance; and Carl Adkins, my village banker, allowed as how I was a reasonably good risk and loaned me a bit more. I thank them warmly. Then, when economic reality became dreary, Saul Landau, Eqbal Ahmad, and Marcus Raskin lifted the sky by supporting my petition to the Trans-National Institute. They thereby gave me space to swing the pen. It is always difficult to write a book, but it is easier if one does not have to fret about paying the bills while one is otherwise unemployed.

# Introduction
# The End of America
# as the Renewable Present

As to politics, we have no past, no future. After
forty-four years of existence under the present
Constitution, what single principle is fixed? . . . We
are as much afloat at sea as the day when the
Constitution went into operation.

—Henry Clay, 1833

One of the central ingredients in the earlier national
mythology was [that] . . . Time was abolished
for God's country. Lifted out of history, free from a
limiting past, Americans were presumably more
self-determining than any other national people had
ever been.

—Loren Baritz, 1964

[Americans] still wish to be *in* but not *of* the
world. . . . They try over and over again, in the
traditional patterns of their culture, to realize what
history seems to indicate cannot be.

—Warren Susman, 1967

The thirteen colonial delegations to the Second Continental Congress voted unanimously on July 2, 1776, that they were, "and of right ought to be, free and independent States." Exactly twelve years later, the government created by those states under the Articles of Confederation and Perpetual Union announced that it had been subverted and overthrown by a group of its own citizens acting in the name of the Constitution of the United States.

The rate of *structural* change promptly dropped almost to zero, and the revolutionary outlook became increasingly conservative: ultimately, indeed, counterrevolutionary. The next effort by Americans to create a new government did not occur for three generations, and it was crushed in a gory four-year war: a veritable human meat grinder— 617,528 dead and at least 375,175 casualties. No further attempt has been made.

Let us stop for a few moments and examine the word I emphasized—*structural*—in order to avoid a misunderstanding about a central theme in this essay.[1] We all know that there have been many changes in America since the adoption of the Constitution. But *structure* is defined as "the arrangement of all the parts of the whole." Thus when I talk about structural change I am speaking about a *re*arrangement of the parts of the whole.

For our purposes, we can concentrate on three parts: the intellectual, the economic, and the political. Both the British Empire (until about 1763) and the Articles of Confederation (see the Appendix) allowed great freedom for the citizens of each unit—the individual colony and state— to develop their own particular arrangement of those elements. If that had not been the case, then we could not talk

[1] To understand what I am trying to do, see Raymond Williams, "Base and Superstructure in Marxist Cultural History," *New Left Review* 82 (Nov.-Dec., 1973), pp. 3–16.

about the cultural differences that emerged between 1620 and 1776. The Articles also provided that those units would act together only under very carefully defined circumstances, and only through specified procedures. No one government could lay down the law for everyone.

But the Constitution created a different arrangement of the parts, and their relationships, and was thus a revolution that produced a structural change. It established the foundation of a superstate, a political giant that had the power to override any single state (or culture). It did so by making population the bedrock of power: a majority could impose its will upon *any* minority.

That inherently—and also practically, as we shall see—subverted the right of people who prefer a different "arrangement of all the parts" to live according to their ideas; and that in turn involved nothing less than the destruction of the ideal underlying the American Revolution of 1776—the revolutionary right of self-determination.

Thus we must at the outset be prepared to face the basic question posed by our revolutionary tradition. Either we believe in the right of self-determination as the basis for creating communities composed of people who come to agree among themselves about "the arrangement of all the parts," or we define the right of self-determination as the basis for some people to project or impose their "arrangement of all the parts" upon everyone else. It is easy to talk about the way other countries violate the first option—about their empires—but if we are to honor our Revolution, then we must talk about the way that we have dishonored our central tradition.

And so to the last part of my effort to clarify what I mean by structural change. When I mentioned "the next effort" to effect such a change, I was of course referring to the secession of the states that created the Confederacy.

17

# WILLIAM APPLEMAN WILLIAMS

They invoked the principle of self-determination to do things that violate some of my fundamental values, but I nevertheless have to confront the issue that I have just defined. I will do so as I discuss the defeat of the Confederate Revolution and the preservation of the Constitutional Revolution.

That outcome serves to underscore the stability of America during a period in which the world underwent many revolutionary changes. But that sense of certainty has been purchased at the cost of much blood and pain, and vast inequities and injustices. There has also been a higher, if more subtle, price: the steady erosion of our commitment to the basic principle of revolutionary self-determination and the continuing distortion of our sense of time and reality. Those processes began very early: if not in the process of colonization, then surely within the first two years after the ratification of the Constitution.

## I

The first Congress of the United States was not organized until April 6, 1789, and George Washington did not take his oath as President for another three weeks. As for the Bill of Rights, it did not become part of the Constitution until December 15, 1791. By that time the world of the Revolutionary Founding Fathers had begun to slip into history. Five days after Washington was inaugurated, the American universe was forever changed by the meeting of the Estates-General in Versailles that accelerated the tempo of the French Revolution. The Bastille was stormed on July 14; a bit later a group of militants, mostly women, forced the King to flee his palace; and by the end of 1791 the French were moving into the kind of social revolution that has never occurred in America.

That upheaval, whatever its tortuous fortunes in

France, defined the essential nature of the world for the next century. The Future had arrived in a Present ostensibly defined and dominated by the American Revolution. Then other revolutions created other Futures. From the outset, and unto this day, therefore, the United States has faced a revolutionary world that increasingly challenged its claim— and self-image—as the dynamic instrument (and symbol) of human fulfillment. That confrontation took many forms and involved various ambiguities, but in the end it became a social, psychological encounter on two levels: between the American idea of America and the reality of America, and between America and the reality of the outer world.

It is useful at the outset, therefore, to clarify the differences between contemporary psychohistory and the classic relationship between psychology and history. The kind of psychohistory that is currently in vogue first appeared about seventy-five years ago and involves the formal and explicit use of psychological and psychiatric theories and insights to explain the actions of individuals and groups. The other relationship goes back at least to Thucydides and involves a process whereby the historian, through his reconstruction and analysis, provides the reader with the sense and feel of a social psychological reality—an understanding of the world view entertained by the people in question.[2]

That ancient approach is essentially dialectical. The purpose is to explore and analyze the ongoing interaction

[2] This tradition has several manifestations. See, for example, the various writings of Rosa Luxemburg; George Lukacs, *History and Class Consciousness* (Cambridge, Mass., M.I.T. Press, 1922, 1967); Jurgen Habermas, *Theory and Practice* (Boston, Beacon Press, 1973); Kenneth E. Boulding, *The Image. Knowledge in Life and Society* (Ann Arbor, Mich., U. of Mich. Press, 1956); and Sheldon S. Wolin, *Politics and Vision* (Boston, Little, Brown, 1960). Though it is not formally concerned with historical problems, the general systems theory that has evolved from the pioneering work of Ludwig von Bertalanffy speaks powerfully to the same issues. See, as a beginning, his *General Systems Theory: Foundations, Development, Applications* (New York, George Braziller, Inc., 1968).

between ideas and reality, and in that way to reveal dysfunctional beliefs, relationships, and behavior that need to be changed in order to honor ideals and generate appropriate action. We now confront such a contradiction. We have struggled so obsessively to preserve the American present, and in the process attempted to control history, that we have distorted our ideals and ceased to deal effectively—let alone creatively—with reality.

America is today irretrievably enmeshed in the breakdown of the Western imperial system that so largely defined world history from Columbus to the end of World War II. The ensuing changes will wrench us out of our accustomed place as the sun around which all else revolves. Far too many people assume, however, that America has always been dynamic, and that the system works, and that therefore the transition will not be especially disturbing or difficult. But an expectation spawned by an illusion is a fantasy.

Consider but two of the fallacies. First, to the extent that the system has worked, it has done so only as an expansionist and imperial system—but imperialism is no longer a viable option. Second, America's dynamism has always been based on *a conception of the future as the present*—as more of the same without any fundamental alterations—but the present is no longer on the agenda. America is going to undergo drastic changes during the next generation.

Most Americans find it difficult to grasp and then come to terms with that reality. Even those who feel it in their bones cannot bring themselves to act in the necessary and appropriate ways. Alexis de Tocqueville was one of the first to perceive the underlying reason for those negative responses. Americans, he noted, "feel no natural inclination for revolutions, but are afraid of them": indeed, they "fear a revolution as the greatest of evils and each of them is inwardly resolved to make great sacrifices to avoid one. In

20

no other country in the world is the love of property keener or more alert . . . and nowhere else does the majority display less inclination toward doctrines which in any way threaten the way property is owned." [3]

By the second decade of the twentieth century, however, a number of Americans had come to realize that the capitalist system itself was posing a visceral threat to the way property was owned and in response turned to the socialism of Eugene Debs. Property in common, they not unreasonably concluded, was better than no property. That challenge was shortly underscored by future-oriented—post-capitalist—revolutions in China, Mexico, and Russia.

The leaders of the American system devised an effective counterattack: repression, reform, and redefinition of property. Though he was not the first to use them, President Woodrow Wilson combined all three in masterly fashion. He exercised all the great power at his disposal against American Socialists, intervened in counterrevolutionary ways in China, Mexico, and Russia, and boldly proposed to re-create the world in the image of the American present. His last public act was to survey "The Road Away From Revolution." The proper route, Wilson explained, was to follow the Christian responsibility "to forego self-interest in order to promote the welfare, happiness, and contentment of others and the community as a whole." [4]

If America had enjoyed a past, a sense of history, that prescription would have been viewed as evidence that Wilson had given up on capitalist reform and embraced Christian Socialism. But lacking any perspective but that of the present, his fellow citizens read his message as Christian Capitalism. In a similar way, they heard Herbert Hoover

[3] *Democracy in America,* translated by G. Lawrence and edited by J. P. Mayer (New York, Doubleday, 1969; originally 1834), pp. 636, 638–39.
[4] *Atlantic Monthly,* Vol. 132 (August, 1923), p. 146.

saying the same thing when he talked so earnestly as a Quaker about the virtues of cooperative capitalism. Which meant that most of them took it this way: Sure, you cooperate and I'll capitalize.

It is easy to dismiss Wilson's political testament as the last musings of a frustrated man. And it is simple to spot the contradictions in Hoover's proposal. But that is to indulge oneself in another kind of fantasy. Wilson and Hoover were going as far as they could to resolve the problem within the limitations of having to work with nothing but the American present.

The corporations were perfectly oriented (and organized) to deal with the problem, and they handled it brilliantly by expanding the American empire abroad while at home redefining property as *disposable and replaceable incidental personal possessions.* Capitalist property had always involved personal possessiveness, but in its classical form it was not irrelevant to the owner as an entrepreneur in the marketplace.[5] The reformulation of the meaning of property began before World War I, steadily gathered momentum during the 1920s (and even during the Great Depression), and came to a highly sophisticated fruition after World War II.

From being an instrument of full citizenship (power) for every man, property became—*and was accepted as*—an instrument of personal pleasure. That consolidated property as power in the hands of a tiny corporate and governmental elite. America became the classic example of corporate state capitalism. The present was preserved. That is the essential meaning of the catechism that the system works.

Until now.

[5] Adam Smith and Karl Marx, as so often, speak to this central point in terms that reinforce each other.

## II

A few perceptive members of the ruling class have a feel for the problem. Thus Henry M. Wriston, an influential member of the policy-making elite, warned as far back as 1961 that Americans must overcome their "nervousness when 'revolution' is mentioned." The American assumption "that all changes in government should be achieved by ballots instead of bullets . . . is a mere wish-fantasy." [6] President John Fitzgerald Kennedy persisted, nevertheless, in his attempt to preserve the present through opening a "New Frontier." And his successors continue that search for a way to sustain the present in the face of the future.

The central problem was clearly (if unintentionally) revealed by Richard B. Morris, an honored historian of the Revolutionary Era. Invoking the "new mystique of world revolution" created by the Founding Fathers, he argued in 1970 that the time had come to make a choice between those who saw the United States "as a counterrevolutionary force that has disavowed her own libertarian traditions" and others like himself who felt "that the values derived from the American Revolutionary experience are still central to the American way of life." [7]

Morris admitted that his formulation was "unfairly oversimplified," but that is not the real issue. The bedrock values of the American Revolution (stated unequivocally in the Declaration of Independence) are the right of revolutionary self-determination and fundamental humanistic equality of *men*. The first has steadily been eroded and the

[6] *Foreign Affairs,* Vol. 39 (1961), pp. 535, 536.
[7] *The Emerging Nations and the American Revolution* (New York, Harper & Row, 1970), pp. x-xii, 40.

second, limited as it is, has never been honored—consider only the First Americans and the Blacks.

To survive we must become revolutionary in two respects: we must admit the past and the future into our lives, and we must change the system so that it enables us to honor our ideals. I think it will help us to examine the way that we Americans responded to a revolutionary world; and I am persuaded that we can then use that knowledge to help us make the changes in our thinking and action that are necessary if we are to regain our freedom and then—finally—create an American commonwealth of regional communities.

# 1

# The Paradoxical Legacy of the Revolution: "Extensive Empire and Self-Government"

Men shall say of succeeding plantacions: the Lord
make it like that of New England: for wee must
Consider that wee shall be as a City upon a Hill, the
eies of all people upon us.
　　　　　　　　　　　　　　　—John Winthrop, 1630

I must indulge a hope that Britain's liberty, as well
as ours, will eventually be preserved by the virtue of
America.
　　—Joseph Warren, Massachusetts revolutionary, 1775

We have it in our power to begin the world again.
　　　　　　　　　　　　　　　—Thomas Paine, 1776

I am persuaded no constitution was ever before as well
calculated as ours for extensive empire and
self-government.
　　　　　　　　　　　　　　　—Thomas Jefferson, 1809

　　Americans emerged from the War for Independence,
the Time of Troubles under the Articles of Confederation,

and the Constitutional Revolution guided by a world view—
a *Weltanschauung*—that was composed of five major elements. All individuals and cultures develop such a way of
making sense of themselves and their environment. No such
overview is perfectly integrated; all reveal square ideas
jimmied into round reality and oval theories awobble in
triangular facts.

In order to function effectively, however, people and
nations attempt to reduce those contradictions and paradoxes
to a minimum. That process can be compared to factoring, a
procedure in mathematics whereby a complex problem is
brought under some measure of control by simplifying it
until the difficulties are clearly understood. That may or may
not lead to a neat and elegant solution, but at least the issues
are clarified.

It is not as easy for people to do that with the various
values and ideas that compose a *Weltanschauung*. But the
effort is made, and the culture functions while coping with
its central paradoxes. Americans evolved a partial accommo-
dation of that kind between 1630 and 1789 that was
characterized by great dynamism and several troublesome
contradictions. Some of the parts of their outlook worked at
cross-purposes with others, and certain values were not
honored in practice.

It is impossible to talk about five things at once and
absurd to try simultaneously to explain how they are brought
into some kind of working relationship. Hence I am going to
factor the problem in this way: I will first define and discuss
three of the components that went into the making of the
American *Weltanschauung* and analyze their interrelation-
ships and consequences. Then I will do the same for the
other two elements. Finally, I will examine the way that
those clusters of values and ideas complemented and con-
tradicted each other, and how they were reconciled around

the theme and reality of expansion. That process will provide a perspective for exploring the American response to a revolutionary world.

# I

Let us begin with these themes: an unqualified commitment to *the right of revolutionary self-determination;* an intense consciousness of *uniqueness;* and a hyperactive sense of *mission.* Americans did not invent either the principle or the practice of independence. The examples of history, including their own as Englishmen, were reinforced by rebellions and uprisings of their own time. The Western world was beginning to erupt after a long period of relative stability, and the unrest reached as far east as Poland and the citizens of Danzig, into English society, and south to Corsica. Many Americans viewed Pascal Paoli, the leader of the struggle in that island, for example, as well as the English radical John Wilkes in London, as an inspiration for their own struggle.

They also drew heavily on the writings of English political philosophers like Algernon Sidney, Thomas Gordon, and John Locke. Most colonials accepted popular uprisings as a natural part of political life and even considered them healthy contributions to the public welfare. But they did not approve, prior to 1770, of "such excesses, as will overturn the whole system of government."[1] British policy pushed them to that line, and their own self-conscious confidence carried them across.

One of the most fascinating aspects of that process involves the way that Americans discussed the issue in terms

[1] Here see Pauline Maier, *From Resistance to Revolution. Colonial Radicals and the Development of American Opposition to Britain, 1765–1766* (New York, Alfred A. Knopf, 1972), pp. 3–24.

of the family. For them, it was a natural metaphor: the family was the center of life and the basis of the larger community; the English monarchy was traditionally thought of within that framework; it was a central theme in the religious rhetoric of the time; and the political economy of mercantilism was based on the principle of mutual obligations and benefits between the English metropolis and the colonies.

It was also a most dynamically useful metaphor.[2] That was apparent as early as 1681, when political philosopher James Tyrell concluded in *Patriarcha non Monarcha* that there was no reason "why a Son when he comes to be a man able to shift for himself, may not in the state of nature marry, and separate himself from his father's Family, even without his Father's consent, if he cannot otherwise obtain his liberty." Having tried all other means to obtain fair treatment from mother Parliament and father King, the colonials began increasingly after 1773 to stress the right of the child to a life of its own. "The day of independent manhood," cried Richard Wells in 1775, "is at hand."

The metaphor of the family, and the early cautions about overturning "the whole system of government," can likewise be seen in the Declaration of Independence.[3] The first two paragraphs, for example, as well as the concluding section, reveal a strong desire to establish the prudence and

[2] Useful for later historians, also, as demonstrated most ably by Edwin G. Burrows and Michael Wallace, "The American Revolution: The Ideology and Psychology of National Liberation," *Perspectives in American History* (Cambridge, Harvard U. Press, 1972), pp. 167–306. The family image becomes apparent upon even the most casual perusal of colonial and Revolutionary correspondence, speeches, and pamphlets. One does not have to interpret it in formal psychological terms, however, to understand its importance.

[3] This should be kept in mind when evaluating Thomas Jefferson's later and oft-quoted remark (1787) that the "tree of liberty must be refreshed from time to time with the blood of patriots and tyrants." Jefferson was not talking about periodic revolutions that changed the structure of government and society; he was far too conservative to advocate that doctrine.

justness of the action. So does the long list of grievances, which are presented as a highly personalized attack upon the King. Be that as it may, the declaration of the principle of revolutionary self-determination was not metaphorical. It was straightforward, bold, and unequivocal.

Men "are endowed by their Creator with certain unalienable rights; that among these are life, liberty, and the pursuit of happiness. . . . Whenever any form of government becomes destructive of these ends, it is the right of the people to alter or to abolish it and to institute new government, laying its foundation on such principles, and organizing its powers in such form, as to them shall seem most likely to effect their safety and happiness." Not only this right, but indeed "their duty, to throw off such government."

James Madison had no hesitation in invoking the right and the duty to justify the movement that he led to subvert the Articles of Confederation. He rested his case on "the transcendent law of nature and of nature's God, which declares that the safety and happiness of society are the objects at which all political institutions aim, and to which all such institutions must be sacrificed." A bit later, in 1792, New Hampshire incorporated the principle into its state constitution: "The doctrine of non-resistance against arbitrary power and oppression is absurd, slavish, and destructive of the good and happiness of mankind." And Thomas Jefferson, who played a key role in drafting the Declaration, subsequently provided a classic summary of the essential doctrine: "every man and body of men on earth possesses the right of self-government."

Later generations reaffirmed the initial commitment. Abraham Lincoln, for example, closely paraphrased the Declaration as part of a resolution he prepared for a meeting in 1852 in support of Hungarian revolutionaries; and Jefferson Davis and other southerners cited it as a major justification for secession. As will become apparent, the right of revolutionary self-determination was so central to the *Weltanschauung* that any hedging or modification always had to be justified with elaborate explanations and reassurances of fidelity to the principle.

## II

The Declaration was in and of itself enough to generate a powerful sense of uniqueness among Americans. That element of the emerging *Weltanschauung* was already well established, however, through the colonial achievement of founding and consolidating a society on the edge of a vast wilderness separated from Europe by a wild reach of treacherous sea. While the deep religious conviction of many colonists colored their expression of uniqueness, there was also a strong secular element in that part of the American consciousness. Thomas Paine best captured that spirit in two classic sentences: one in *Common Sense*, "We have it in our power to begin the world again"; and another near the end of 1776, "Not a place upon earth might be so happy as America."

The assumption of most colonists that they were purifying the very special tradition of the Rights of Free Englishmen likewise strengthened their awareness of being unique. Others saw America as "the last and greatest theater for the improvement of mankind," and "for all ages to come a chosen seat of Freedom, Arts, and Heavenly Knowledge; which are now either drooping or dead in those countries of the old world." As the reference to Heavenly Knowledge suggests, however, the pre-Revolutionary sense of uniqueness was thoroughly infused with religious exultation.

Perry Miller summarized that dominant theme in one perceptive remark: "for Americans, the exercise of liberty becomes simply the one true obedience to God." [4] A few particularly enthusiastic citizens declared that the Revolution was the golden link in God's great chain of being, one destined to create the *"Millennial State."* Most were less ecstatic, more inclined like John Adams to view the upheaval "as merely the opening of a grand scheme and design in Providence for the illumination of the ignorant, and the emancipation of the slavish part of mankind all over the earth." Even Jonathan Edwards, whose respect for the power and the rigor of the Lord made him cautious in such matters, allowed that it was possible that He "might in it begin a new world in a spiritual respect."

Victory in the war, and the subsequent replacement of the Articles with the Constitution, further strengthened that already intense consciousness of being unique. The Lord in His wisdom, concluded Ezra Stiles, eighteenth-century astronomer and President of Yale, will raise America "high above all nations which He has made, in numbers, and in praise, and in name, and in honor." The religious formulation continued to be employed by subsequent observers. Andrew Jackson declared, for example, that God had charged the United States with the unique responsibility of preserving freedom "for the benefit of the human race." And, along with Lincoln and others, Ralph Waldo Emerson thought that the Civil War made it clear that "our whole history appears like a last effort of the Divine Providence in behalf of the human race."

That view was sustained into the twentieth century, perhaps most notably by William McKinley and Woodrow

---

[4] Perry Miller, "From the Covenant to the Revival," in J. W. Smith and A. L. Jamison, *The Shaping of American Religion.* Vol. I. *Religion in American Life* (Princeton, N.J., Princeton U. Press, 1961), p. 332. Also see U. O. Hatch, "The Origins of Civil Millennialism in America: New England Clergymen, War with France, and the Revolution," *William and Mary Quarterly,* Vol. 31 (1974), pp. 407–430.

Wilson. But from about the time of the war against Mexico (1846–48) it came to be invoked less as a confident explanation of America's special nature than as a justification for actions which seemed clearly to violate other values and ideas inherent in the *Weltanschauung*. The shift toward the secular argument began with the formulation and adoption of the Constitution. Most Americans, whether initially in favor of or opposed to that change, considered its substance and theory to involve a true innovation in the political history of mankind. And there was, for that matter, some validity to the claim.

Classical political theory, symbolized for the Revolutionary generation by Montesquieu, was founded on one axiom: representative government could not survive in a large state (or empire). The bigger the nation, the greater the centralization, consolidation, and tyranny of power. Men could govern themselves only as citizens of a relatively small community. But guided by the genius of Madison, the makers of the Constitution turned that theory on its head. The larger the sphere, he explained, the sounder the foundation for freedom and representative government. "The question is," he explained, "whether small or extensive republics are more favorable to the election of proper guardians of the public weal; and it is clearly decided in favor of the latter."

It was an intellectual revolution, and one that left some Americans uneasy throughout the subsequent history of the United States. But it unquestionably provided a secular cornerstone for the doctrine of uniqueness. One farmer caught the spirit of those who approved in a joyful letter of appreciation to Madison. "America may rejoice, and plume herself in the idea of having made the Rent in the great curtain that withheld the light from human nature—by her exertions she let day and the Rights of Man become legible and intelligible to a Shakkled World."

Jefferson's famous assertion in his first Inaugural Address that America was "the world's best hope" was intimately related to another passage in the same speech. Our success, he explained, "furnishes new proof of the falsehood of Montesquieu's doctrine, that a republic can be preserved only in a small territory. The reverse is the truth." Jefferson never ceased being ecstatic. "I am persuaded," he wrote Madison in 1809, that "no constitution was ever before as well calculated as ours for extensive empire and self-government." Five years later he concluded that it "has rendered useless almost everything written before on the structure of government."

That intellectual lode was mined as if it were inexhaustible. Emerson called the Constitution "the hope of the world." William Henry Seward, Governor of New York, Senator, and later Secretary of State, viewed its adoption as "the most important secular event in the history of the human race." The same kind of logic led Lincoln to declare that America was "the last best hope of earth." A century later, President Harry S. Truman confidently asserted that "all the world knows that the fate of civilization depends, to a very large extent, on what we do." Long before that vehement reaffirmation of uniqueness, however, the confidence that America was special had become deeply entangled with the conviction that America was charged with a singular mission.

## III

All cultures view themselves as distinctive in some respects and to that degree are mindful of a mission to develop and honor their differences. And a significant number have been so confident of the value of their peculiarities that they have been active missionaries to a large congregation.

But Edward McNall Burns is correct in concluding that, "to a greater extent than most other people, Americans have conceived of their nation as ordained in some extraordinary way to accomplish great things in the world." [5]

As with its sense of uniqueness, the roots of the American conviction of its mission and destiny lie deep in the religiosity of the early colonists. John Winthrop was dedicated to the proposition that the establishment of a true church in Massachusetts would be the first and necessary step in saving England. And long before the Revolution the northern colonies, as Perry Miller observes, were "thoroughly accustomed to conceiving of themselves as a chosen race." John Cushing, Ezra Stiles, and Timothy Dwight were typical of those who constantly reiterated that theme. [6] More revealing, perhaps, was Jacob Duché's crusading cry of encouragement to the members of the Continental Congress: "Go on, ye chosen band of Christians."

Not all of those worthies were Christians, of course, but the Old Testament glories of Israel provided an idiom that united the orthodox with their Deistic comrades. Samuel Cooper of New England exploited that imagery, and foresaw "astounding dispensations" for America. Jefferson followed his contributions to the Declaration of Independence with the proposal that the official insignia of the new nation depict the Children of Israel being led ever forward by a shaft of light from the heavens. His entry was not adopted, but "The Great Seal" on the one-dollar bill is drawn from the same tradition.

The religious element survived longer as an overt part of America's consciousness of mission than as a component of

[5] *The American Idea of Mission. Concepts of National Purpose and Destiny* (Westport, Ct., Greenwood Press, 1957), pp. vii, 5.
[6] In addition to Miller's work, see Albert K. Weinberg, *Manifest Destiny* (Baltimore, The Johns Hopkins Press, 1935), pp. 39–42.

34

its sense of uniqueness. God in all his many forms has been invoked in every American confrontation with the world after the initial attack on the Popish Church of England: the "licentious" French, the Black Catholics of Latin America, the infidels of Turkey, Islam, and Asia, and the atheistic Reds of modern times. Even Seward, a most worldly man, thought it wise to underwrite his secular expansionism with the imperatives of "a Higher Law" and references to America as "a new and further development of the Christian System."

Perhaps the most revealing formulations appeared as the nation, in the face of increasingly severe domestic divisions, began to question its uniqueness. Representative John Wentworth of Illinois admitted those doubts at the beginning of 1845, but nevertheless reasserted the destiny. He "did not believe that the God of Heaven, when he crowned the American arms with success [in the Revolution], designed that the original States should be the only abode of liberty on earth. On the contrary, he only designed them as the great center from which civilization, religion, and liberty should radiate until the whole continent shall bask in their blessing."

Then, at the end of that year, the sense of mission was formulated in a ringing paragraph of confidence and exhortation. Two days after Christmas, John L. O'Sullivan of the New York *Morning News* wrote himself into the hearts of most of his countrymen and into every history book. America's mission was beyond discussion: "It is our *manifest destiny* to overspread and to possess the whole of the continent which Providence has given us for the development of the great experiment of liberty and federative self-government entrusted to us."

For a moment, at least, that supercharged evangelicalism rolled back the doubts even of Herman Melville. He had just finished a revealing and troubled account ( *Typee,* 1846) of his seduction by life in the South Pacific. He was confessing, in his way, the American Mortal Sin. He had lost his heart to a beautiful brown woman and in the process had been forced to question whether America was indeed the best of all possible worlds. Four years later, in *White Jacket,* he seemingly recanted. "We Americans are the peculiar, chosen people—the Israel of our time; we bear the ark of the liberties of the world. . . . God has predestined. . . . The rest of the nations must be in our rear."

In that passage, at any rate, Melville was typical of many Americans who, while deeply religious, generally shied away from formally invoking the Lord's Name as the prime mover of the nation's mission to save mankind. They developed their own idiom even before the Revolution. America, wrote one, "bids the fairest of any to promote *the perfection and happiness of mankind.*" Another agreed: the colonies would become "the foundation of a great and mighty empire, the largest the world ever saw to be founded on such principles of liberty and freedom."

Other Revolutionary leaders like Arthur Lee and Samuel Adams simply assumed that America must carry the torch to Scotland, Ireland, Canada, and even France. Employing his usual magic with words, Jefferson concluded a bit later that "old Europe will have to lean on our shoulders, and to hobble along by our side." Any and all American expansion shortly became, in the idiom of Andrew Jackson and James K. Polk, a glorious exercise in extending "the area of freedom." Even Orestes Brownson, one of the most perceptive critics of midnineteenth-century America, could argue that reforming the country was a preliminary step in claiming the rightful "hegemony of the world."

Brownson provides a particularly illuminating insight into the peculiar nature of the developing sense of mission. He displayed considerable condescension toward Latin

Americans—and even other whites in Canada. "The work of civilization," he callously remarked in 1866, "could go on without them as well as with them." The overt racial national superiority—and in many cases outright racism—was an integral part of America's consciousness of mission from the first years of colonization. The Africans taken into slavery and the Indians dispossessed of their lands were viewed as beings to be saved by Americans.

Nor were they the only ones defined as inferiors to be brought along into righteousness and civilization. Revolutionary leaders like John Dickinson and Samuel Adams displayed open disgust—if not contempt—for most Englishmen: They had failed to make a revolution and then lost their chance for a dispensation by not subverting the Father's assault upon the children. That attitude was classically expressed by Jefferson in his early (but not published) draft of the Declaration of Independence. So also women: they were honored, but not included in the commitment to self-determination—or treated as equal partners in the struggle to fulfill America's unique mission. Women did participate more extensively and routinely in many aspects of life in those years than they did through most of the nineteenth and twentieth centuries, but it was nevertheless a white male world.

Thomas Jefferson was perceptive and honest enough to recognize and acknowledge those harsh truths. He squirmed and side-slipped his way among them throughout his life. He enjoyed the company of the more liberated upper-class women of France, but felt more at ease with the American female who tended hearth and home. And, along with many other southerners of his generation, he was deeply troubled by slavery. But the moral imperative of emancipation was always checked by the power of the arguments about social upheaval and economic disaster. That balance of forces paralyzed them, and slavery survived into the era when American cotton fed the textile mills of England. Jefferson told us in one memorable sentence, however, about the chill in their souls: "Indeed, I tremble for my country when I reflect that God is just."

## IV

Jefferson's anguished foreboding bespoke a sense of isolation that went beyond the questions involving women, Indians, and Black slaves. That is not difficult to understand. The conviction of uniqueness and mission and the commitment to revolutionary self-determination inevitably created *a deep sense of aloneness—of isolation.* That is the fourth theme of the American *Weltanschauung.* From the beginning, some Americans accepted that condition as basically desirable, and formulated a philosophy and a policy that much later came mistakenly to be known as isolationism. But even that outlook contained a strong element of expansionism: at first to control the North American continent (otherwise known as the Western Hemisphere), and then to dominate the world marketplace. Even so, their view was and remained a less aggressive conception of America. And, during various periods, it exerted a significant influence on policy decisions.

But most Americans always dealt with their awareness of being alone in a far different way. The elements that initially created the sense of aloneness were reinforced during the Constitutional Revolution by the deep consciousness of having turned conventional political theory on its head. The Founding Fathers were keenly aware that they were challenging the wisdom of the gods: empire inherently destroyed self-government. Yet on they plunged into empire.

One does not need a degree in psychiatry to hear the note of desperate hope in Jefferson's bold assertion of the revolutionary theory in his first Inaugural: "[Our success] furnishes new proof of the falsehood of Montesquieu's doctrine, that a republic can be preserved only in a small territory. The reverse is the truth."

Those ideological and psychological components of the sense of isolation were initially reinforced by geography and the time lag in communications (including the transmission of technology). The development and institutionalization of industrialism in England underscored the backwardness and weakness of America's agrarian-commercial political economy. That disparity was ultimately overcome in a way that confirmed the early feelings of uniqueness, mission, and aloneness. For, as America replaced Britain as the world's greatest industrial power, it experienced the isolation of superiority just as it had earlier suffered the isolation of inferiority.

From the outset, moreover, America's *Weltanschauung* generated a particularly disturbing—and potentially terrifying—kind of aloneness: *isolation in Time*. To grasp the nature of this phenomenon, we have to break free of our workaday perception of Time. We normally think in terms of the clock and the calendar. Let us call that time with a small *t*. But, at various stages in our lives, and in our development as a culture, we think in terms of the past, the present, and the future. That is time with a capital *T*.

The capital *T* kind of Time invariably produces all kinds of abberrations for those who lack a sense of history and of process. By defining themselves as unique and isolated, the Revolutionary Fathers rapidly lost their awareness of history and process. They had studied history, perhaps more than any other generation of Americans, but then they cut themselves off from it and thereby became trapped in the Present.

They killed Time (and History) in the name of uniqueness. They concluded that the Past was Bad and that the Future would very likely be Bad, and hence all that remained was the Here and Now. If you have a philosophical turn of mind, you see the point immediately: Americans were the first existentialists—to live now is all, over and over and over again. Forever, as it were, without any Amen. Perhaps, indeed, America is best defined by an existential sense of omnipotence. Our purpose is to preserve the Present forever.

Long before the Revolution, the colonists began to damn the Past. There was nothing good, or even human, for example, in Turkey, France, Egypt, India, Spain, or Russia. Even England was a corrupt society that had to be saved by America. They considered themselves to be a new people, and those few among them who viewed Americans as ordinary mortals temporarily graced by nature were considered subversive. America was regenerating what little was good in the Past, adding its special and major contribution, and preserving it against the Future.

Emerson encapsulated some of that outlook in his remark that "whatever is old corrupts, and the past turns to snakes." As usual, Melville saw deeper into the issue. "America must free herself from time, from the past, in order to be what she must be." Others concentrated on the problem of the Future. John Adams was only one of many who grew increasingly uneasy about losing the golden Present to what they considered the subversive forces of luxury and equality. A bit later, Jackson and Polk provided a classic formulation: the Indians had to be removed, the Blacks controlled, and the Mexicans disciplined by war so that the *one* area of freedom could be preserved and extended into the Future.

## V

This determination to cope with being alone by preserving and expanding the present—by defying Time—was reinforced by the awareness of internal differences and conflicts that threatened the sense of uniqueness. That consciousness defined the fifth component of the emerging *Weltanschauung*. Most early Americans talked openly and routinely about the reasons for—and the probabilities of—separation into two or more regional confederations, and about class antagonisms. The upper classes worried constantly about the demands from below for more democracy and equality. That pressure, which created a similar tension between the middle and lower classes (to say nothing of the slaves and the masters), was a regular part of American life that periodically erupted into violence.

Those fundamental internal threats to American uniqueness (and hence its mission) were contained by several forces. First, the commonly shared sense of uniqueness, mission, and isolation operated as a deterrent among those who wanted—and needed—changes. Second, the unusual ability, presence, and performance of the leaders of the Revolutionary and Constitutional generation generated a basic sense of trust and respect that likewise served to limit most agitation. Third, the upper class displayed a willingness to accept reform if it was undertaken slowly and if it honored the basic commitment to the values that defined America's uniqueness.

Fourth, when the demands for reform did occasionally cross the line into rebellion, the upper class possessed superior firepower because of their control of the state and federal governments, and they displayed no hesitation in using it to preserve the unique American present. In those situations, furthermore, the general consciousness of unique-

41

ness, mission, and isolation weakened the spirit of the rebels.

Finally, the commitment to an expansionist political economy did function, as Madison argued, to defuse internal differences and conflicts. It provided a surplus of resources (and hence opportunity) and a vast space that made it extremely difficult to organize a social movement that involved people throughout the empire. That was such a crucial element in the American outlook that it deserves separate consideration.

# VI

Expansion lies at the center of the American *Weltanschauung*. It was and remains the key to resolving the visceral problems created by the sense of uniqueness, the commitment to mission, and the way out of being isolated —of being alone. A poet named Frederick Jackson Turner said it once and forever: the frontier, the West, has been "a gate of escape." He truly understood the American idiom: √ the only way to preserve the Present is to recreate it into infinity. Or, to translate Turner into the idiom of Time, the only way to kill the Past and the Future is to stay in the Present. And to do that, one needs first a continent, then a hemisphere, next the world, and finally the universe—or at least a galaxy. Neil Armstrong said more than he knew when he stepped down on the moon and remarked that it was a giant step for mankind. America has always considered itself as mankind, and hence the Present was once again secure. The moon, as John Fitzgerald Kennedy put it, was merely another New Frontier.

The consciousness of America as an endlessly expanding frontier is the product of many forces. It is as silly to try to reduce them to one eternal primary reason as it is to play pool on the assumption that all you have to do is to sink one ball at a time. The key to understanding history also works in the lock of comprehending a pool game: the crucial thing is to see it as a unitary—a holistic—experience that makes sense only as one integrates certain immutable factors in eternally—yet limited—changing patterns.

We lose the pool game, and we become dysfunctional as a people, unless we transform the particular and disparate elements of reality into a coherent whole. The American calculus, our version of the fundamental way to integrate the parts into the whole, has always hinged on expansion. We have never mustered the wisdom to say at some point that enough is enough. We have always been busy preserving the Present.

First there was the continent, and our forefathers, driven by a mission, soon established their superior power. They were simultaneously pushed forward by the acquisitive, possessive individualism of the capitalist ethic. And those elemental forces, idealistic and materialistic, were perfectly joined together in the theory that empire was the only way to honor avarice and morality. The only way to be good *and* wealthy. The only way to preserve the Present.

Expanding the marketplace enlarged the area of freedom. Expanding the area of freedom enlarged the marketplace. Both preserved America's uniqueness against the insidious forces of the Past and the Future. And thereby honored the mission to transform the world. And so would end the terrifying sense of aloneness and isolation.

So it seemed and so it has been believed. But the killing of the Past and the Future in the name of the Present, the perfect and wholly justifiable crime, ultimately ceased to be the way to turn the dream into reality. It proved to be a nightmare that yet defines our waking hours. The challenge is to recover our Past so that we can then imagine and create our Future.

**43**

# 2

# The First Ally Poses
# the First Challenge

The French Revolution drew a red-
hot plough share through the history of
America as well as through that of France.
> —Colonel Stephen Higginson,
> Revolutionary leader from Massachusetts, c. 1800

I presume there are not to be found five
men in Europe who understand the nature
of liberty and the theory of government
so well as they are understood by five
hundred men in America.
> —Joel Barlow, New England chaplain,
> lawyer and entrepreneur, 1788

Too many Frenchmen, like too many Americans,
pant for equality of persons and property.
> —John Adams, 1790

What is liberty when one class of men can
starve another? What is equality when the

rich man by his monopoly exercises the right of life
and death over his fellow man?
> —Jacques Roux, French revolutionary, speaking
> in Paris, 1793

All of the miseries of mankind have arisen
from freemen not maintaining and exercising
their own sentiments.
> —Pennsylvania mechanic, 1784

All other republicanism is a cheat.
> —*Kentucky Gazette*, 1795

Our new fellow citizens [in Louisiana]
are as yet incapable of self-government as children.
> —Thomas Jefferson, 1803

Despite all that has been written about the Great
Atlantic Revolution that ostensibly involved the United
States and Western Europe in a common experience,[1] the
French Revolution that erupted in 1788–89 was significantly
different from the earlier upheaval that created the United
States. Americans did not initially recognize the disparity
and hence responded enthusiastically to the news from Paris.
Not only were they flattered by the easy conclusion that
their example had caused the events in France, but they
eagerly viewed the French Revolution as ending their isolation. They excitedly assumed that the old ally against Great
Britain had become a new ally against the Past—that America was no longer isolated in the Present.

Americans rather quickly realized the flaws in that

---

[1] For a sophisticated statement of this interpretation, see Jacques Godechot,
*France and the Atlantic Revolution of the Eighteenth Century, 1770–1799*
(New York, Free Press, 1965).

analysis, however, and their increasing perception of the issues produced a serious division within the country. One group identified strongly with the French people—women as well as men—who sought to create a republicanism that honored the ideas and traditions of popular sovereignty and the worker—*"le social."* Others feared precisely those objectives. It seemed, at least for a time, that there might be a third American revolution more influenced by events in France than developments in France were guided by the American example. In the end, however, Americans resolved their differences by reasserting their uniqueness and superiority, by acting on their theory of expansion, and being cowed by their fear of the Future. America remained isolated.

Nothing dramatized that reality more effectively than the drastically different priorities of the two revolutions.[2] The French moved first to reorder domestic society, to change its *structure;* the Americans acted primarily to preserve what they had created. The French accepted their Past and sought to adapt and honor its best traditions; the Americans sought to escape the Past. Millions of French people were hungry; most Americans were not. The French acknowledged violence as a part of revolution; Americans denied and sublimated their violence by projecting it upon those they defined as inferiors.

The French attacked institutionalized religion; Americans opened the back door to religious politics. The French become expansionist largely in response to counterrevolutionary attacks from outside; the Americans became imperial

[2] I am aware of the fluctuations within the French Revolution, and the struggle for power among the various groups and factions. I am speaking here of the fundamental thrust of the revolution from 1789 to 1800. On this point see Edward Hallett Carr, "The Russian Revolution: Its Place in History," in *The October Revolution* (New York, Vintage Books, 1971), pp. 1–53.

as a matter of principle. And, finally, the French struggled to destroy feudalism, whereas Americans constructed a tortured ideology to prove that they had no feudal past because slavery was not feudalism. They thus sought to evade the truth that slavery was the American equivalent of feudalism which exercised a similar power over American society and its development.

Small wonder, then, that the cry of "Liberty, Fraternity, Equality" echoed louder and further down the corridors of Time and Power than the American demand for independence and empire. For what one does with independence becomes crucial to the existence of independence. Nor should there be any mystery about the insight of one contemporary American, Colonel Stephen Higginson, who declared, "The French Revolution drew a red-hot plough share through the history of America as well as through that of France."

# I

The key to that perception lies in another: the effort to preserve the Present inexorably drives one into an embrace with the status quo. Americans moved in accordance with that logic even as they won their independence. As the ideal of a mercantilistic mutuality of obligation and rewards was beginning to slide into oblivion, the British Board of Trade concluded in 1721 that it was "inconvenient" and "disorderly" to allow colonial assemblies to exercise too much power. Most colonial-Revolutionary Americans soon came to agree: pure democracy was troublesome and dangerous, and hence the people could rightfully and properly speak and act only through their representatives.[3]

---

[3] Here see, among others, Roy N. Lokken, "The Concept of Democracy in Colonial Political Thought," *William and Mary Quarterly,* Vol. 16 (1959), pp. 568–580.

Given that outlook, the beginnings of the French Revolution appeared auspicious. The New York *Journal,* commenting on the July, 1788, demand of the nobles to be recognized as legitimate spokesmen, concluded that they had "imbibed a spirit of liberty into their minds" from the United States. The *Gazette of the United States* happily reported a bit later that the Truth was expanding from America "throughout the world." It was, in the view of the Massachusetts *Sentinel,* "one of the greatest Revolutions recorded in the annals of time." Even George Washington, a most conspicuously prudent and conservative man, greeted it with "enthusiasm."

Some of that sympathy and support flowed from the gratitude which Americans felt for the crucial aid that France had supplied between 1776 and 1783, and from the related feeling that a reinvigorated and regenerated France would serve as a check to England's growing economic and military power. But most of it was generated by America's commitment to the right of revolutionary self-determination (and the feeling that France would use that right properly), and the dedication to the mission of destroying the bad old Past and extending the good American Present. Thomas Jefferson and other Americans might occasionally dream of isolating themselves from the evils of the rest of the world and perfect their City on the Hill, but their fears and their expansionism routinely obscured that vision.[4] Jefferson revealed the basic attitude in his observation that "the liberty of the whole earth was depending on the issue."

Most people did not think that America could survive alone in the good Present. The *Kentucky Gazette* bluntly acknowledged that fear: "the happiness, liberties, and the

[4] See, for example, Jefferson to G. K. van Hogendorp, October 13, 1785: *The Papers of Thomas Jefferson,* ed. by Julian P. Boyd (Princeton: Princeton U. Press, 1953), Vol. 8, pp. 631–634.

prosperity of America, depend on the success of that [French] republic." The New York *Journal* agreed that all would be well if the French grasped "that heavenly jewel which we so justly prize." And some enthusiasts thought that America and France would together usher in the millennium: "Mankind will throw away the weapons of death. . . . Over all earth perpetual peace will diffuse her heavenly joys, and all grief and mourning will be buried in endless oblivion."

Such enthusiasm led most Americans to view the early violence in France as the limited kind of protest that was sometimes necessary to make rulers responsible to public needs. And the proclamation of the Republic on September 21, 1792, generated an excitement that generally overrode the great concern about the subsequent execution of Louis XVI. The *Kentucky Gazette*, for example, initially expressed outrage over "the infernal assassination" by "a base and cowardly faction," but shortly concluded that the Old Regime had brought such extreme measures upon itself. And others who decried the action acknowledged "the general fact that the French people have the right to choose whatever form of government admits of no doubt."

The involvement of the lower orders in cities like Paris and Marseilles, and the related radicalization of the Revolution, encouraged those Americans who were growing increasingly upset about economic and social developments at home. The first wave of demonstrations in favor of the Republic, typified by the Civic Feast in Boston on January 24, 1793, involved people of all classes and reached into the South as well as affecting the North and West. Those gatherings, as well as the outpourings of poems and broadsides, revealed a deep sense of identity and commitment to the French upheaval. One toast in Kentucky caught the spirit perfectly: "Freedom in every Nation in every age."

Within that framework, however, many Americans began to agitate for changes at home. They identified with the spirit of the *sans-culottes*, and raised the same issues that Jacques Roux formulated in his speech to the radicals of Paris: "What is liberty when one class of men can starve another? What is equality when the rich man by his monopoly exercises the right of life and death over his fellow man?" That kind of social anger had been present in America since at least the 1740s, and the policies of Alexander Hamilton and President Washington had revived and extended such antagonism during the years when the French Revolution became more radical.

A resolution adopted in 1791 by dissenters in Pittsburgh, for example, protested the "undue advantage" being taken by the few "of the ignorance and necessities of others," and bitterly attacked policies whereby "the liberty, property, and even the morals of the people are sported with, to gratify particular men in their ambitions and interested measures." Such ferment was intensified and extended by the 1791 excise tax on whiskey, and overt resistance rapidly developed in the South (particularly in North Carolina) and in western Pennsylvania.

That was the situation—indeed, it was a tinderbox— when on April 8, 1793, Edmond Charles Genêt arrived in the United States as the Minister of the French Republic. He immediately lit his first match by forgoing his title in favor of being addressed—in the idiom of the Revolution— as simply Citizen Genêt. He also began to commission privateers to help France fight the counterrevolutionary forces led by Great Britain and generally encouraged the public opposition to the Washington Administration.

The President responded with a proclamation of neutrality and shortly thereafter sent John Jay to England to negotiate a settlement of outstanding territorial and commercial issues. It was as if he had pumped the bellows upon Genêt's flickering flame. Domestic tensions and enthusiasm for the French Revolution combined to create a political and social turmoil. Democratic Societies, more than forty of them, spread throughout the country with the speed of a forest fire exploding along the treetops. People proudly addressed each other as Citizen upon the streets and in the taverns, and workingmen became increasingly militant. "All of the miseries of mankind," exclaimed a Philadelphia mechanic, "have arisen from freemen not maintaining and exercising their own sentiments."

Becoming ever more disturbed about "the discord and anarchy," Washington first demanded the recall of Genêt. Then, in response to overt resistance to the whiskey tax in Pennsylvania, he ordered an army into the field and denounced the Democratic Societies. They were guilty of trying "to form *their will* into laws for the government of the whole"—clearly the kind of direct democracy that threatened the uniqueness and mission of America. Washington survived that crisis, and the one created by the highly unfavorable terms of the treaty which Jay had accepted in London, because most Americans proved unwilling to risk the Present for the Future.

## II

For that matter, ever more of them came to feel that the French Revolution was actually delaying the progress of the world into the good American Present. Washington's progressively negative view of the Revolution is not surprising, for he never wanted to overthrow the existing *structure* of society. Nor can his sense of America's unique mission be questioned. His Farewell Address, after all, is essentially a plea not to be distracted from the primary objective. Do not, he warned, allow internal differences, attractions or animosities toward other nations, or temporary weakness, to take the form of a Pied Piper charming America back into a Bad Past or forward into a chimerical Future. His counsel was simple and unequivocal: patience until we are strong, and then we can guarantee and expand the American Present.

Similar views of the French were expressed by Gouverneur Morris, John Adams, and Joel Barlow. Barlow noted in his diary on October 3, 1788, for example, that "there are not to be found five men in Europe who understand the nature of liberty and the theory of government so well as they are understood by five hundred men in America." But he nevertheless acknowledged the French right to go to hell in their own way. "Different constitutions of government are necessary to the different societies on the face of this planet." A tailor in Greece or China "would not have many customers either in London or Paris."

Morris, the conservative representative of the United States in Paris, dismissed events in France as the product of "all that romantic spirit and all those romantic ideas of government which, happily for America, we were cured of before it was too late." The French were to be pitied: they "adopted experiment instead of experience, and wander in the dark because they prefer lightning to light." Adams was characteristically blunt. The French were full of "solemn hypocricy"—"like too many Americans, [they] pant for equality of persons and property."

Though he was very cautious about expressing his views publicly because of his desire to maintain his political support among those who continued to sympathize with the French, Jefferson was also skeptical. The French, he commented in 1787, are "incapable of any serious effort but under the word of command." In subsequent years, Jefferson repeatedly advised the French to go slow, to copy America, even as he doubted the ability to recognize his wisdom. "The comparison of our government with those of Europe is like a comparison of heaven and hell." The French were clearly not ready for the American Present: a dictatorship might well be appropriate, at the least "a constitutional monarchy." In some respects, even at that early date, the Past began to seem less challenging to the Present than the Future.

Madison agreed that the assault on property revealed a "licentiousness" that threatened America's opportunity to rewrite political theory and consolidate its imperial Present. Militant social solidarity, particularly among the lower orders, was something that Madison had invested much time and energy to thwart. That note, and the others in the same chord, had been sounded as early as 1787 by those who attacked the French for utopianism: it "cannot succeed," and leads only to "licentiousness, rapine, and free-booting." Empire was the key to property, and property was the foundation of the good American Present.

Despite their complaints, and their agitation through the Democratic Societies, most Americans proved unwilling to challenge that syllogism. Particularly if the property was available. The ensuing criticism of French bloodletting and irreligion revealed much of America's uneasiness about its own actions. Americans did not like to confront violence as a central issue of life simply because they so regularly used it against nature and their fellow human beings. Violence in the service of the Present became virtuous, even religious; but violence in the name of the Future was the irreligious work of "brigands" and "gangs of robbers."

Editors in Boston and Kentucky agreed that "all other republicanism is a cheat." And a writer in Connecticut chronicled what he considered to be the failure of the French Revolution with as much sadness as bitterness.

53

"Nor can it, alas! be said that 'regeneration' has made France any better for us." That pronoun tells it all: the central concern about self-determination involved not the French and their Revolution, but its impact on America.

Jefferson spoke for many when he commented privately in 1801 that the Revolution "was long over." That judgment was not simply, nor even primarily, based on the French challenge to American commerce, or to the coup d'état of November 9, 1799, that elevated Napoleon Bonaparte to supreme power. Jefferson could hardly complain about that, since he had earlier judged it to be wholly in keeping with the French inability to copy America. Rather, as the remark indicated, most Americans concluded that the Revolution ended when the French failed to follow the jewel of an example provided by the United States. Napoleon became the convenient object upon which to vent that frustration and deepened sense of isolation.

A few discerning observers, such as the editor of the *Independent Chronicle,* recognized the long-term benefits of the Revolution: the economic improvement; the firm foundation for civil rights; the weakening of feudal and clerical institutions; the establishment of a tradition of popular sovereignty; and the social solidarity among the lower orders. But the general reaction sometimes reached the point of hysteria. "Fickle people," spat the Baltimore *American;* "what a degrading picture they present to the world." They were not even "fitted to receive a rational government." The restoration of the Bourbons was welcomed: "It is not a *counter revolution,* but it is a *revolution.*" Or, as Morris explained, "the long agony is over."

What had happened involved a subtle but subversive modification of the commitment to the principle of revolutionary self-determination. The axiom itself was vigorously reasserted, of course, by Washington as well as Jefferson, and

54

by Adams and Morris as well as James Monroe and Albert Gallatin. "We certainly cannot deny to other nations the principle whereon our own government stands"; "everyone has a right to form and adopt whatever government they like best to live under"; and America is committed to "the equal and unalienable rights of man." But those who were not yet wise enough to define self-determination in terms of the American Present would have to suffer the opprobrium (and even the enmity) of the United States for mistakenly cherishing parts of the Past or reaching foolishly for the Future.

# III

Such disapprobation could be most consequential, particularly if one was black, red, brown, or living athwart the path of America's uniquely missionary expansionism. The Blacks in the French West Indies were, after the slaves and the Red People in America, the first to learn that painful lesson. The French Revolution moved almost immediately westward across the Atlantic to Santo Domingo. The colored freemen and women rose in rebellion and were then joined by the slaves. That was viscerally disturbing to many Americans, northern as well as southern. Washington, "sincerely regretting" the uprising, allowed himself to be "happy" to help restore order. Jefferson agreed. He emphasized the danger that American commerce might be captured by Great Britain, but he quietly acknowledged the threat of a Black Republic.

Then the French abolished slavery, and southerners led the denunciation of such "diabolical decrees." The French were not at all reassuring about the inferiority of the Blacks: "These men may be killed," reported French General Victor Leclerc, "but they will not surrender. They laugh at death;—

and it is the same with the women." What happened next is forever tangled in the entrails of commerce, fear of Blacks, and expansionist avarice.

Jefferson is reported to have told the French that "nothing would be easier than to furnish your army and fleet, and to reduce [Black leader] Toussaint to starvation." The account is ambiguous; and, even if taken as valid, must be discounted as part of Jefferson's passion to acquire Florida and the western half of the continent. But even Dumas Malone, his most exhaustive and sympathetic biographer, allowed that "Bonaparte was warranted in assuming that the expedition to St. Domingo would arouse no American objection." The conclusion is inescapable: Revolutionary self-determination for Blacks was either a reversion to primitivism or a leap forward into the furthest frontiers of the Future.

Northern traders fondled their prejudices with one hand while with the other fingered the possibility of joining Great Britain to dominate the commerce of the island. Noble Toussaint never had a chance. Jefferson ultimately came to view him as a pawn in his own maneuvers to acquire Louisiana, but even that condescension came too late. Toussaint died as a prisoner of the French. The first American intervention in Santo Domingo pointed the way to those which followed during the next two centuries. The right of revolutionary self-determination proved in practice to be applicable only if it led to an acceptance of the American Present.

Haiti somehow evaded that fate—at least for a time. It won its independence on January 1, 1804, as the first Black nation of modern times. But not recognition by the United States. Gallatin, one hopes, was ashamed of his feeble arguments against that action. But John Quincy Adams, the son of John, subversively educated by his mother Abigail, argued for recognition. He was no doubt influenced by his desire for trade as well as a concern to honor his moral imperatives; but the commerce could be had without allowing a Black official to attend White House functions, and so Adams lost the battle. Haiti ultimately refused (in 1826–27) to continue the charade and cut American trade to the bone. Adams bided his time and devised a clever counterattack. He used petitions to improve commercial relations to argue for recognition and at the same time to criticize American slaveowners who resisted that course.

Jefferson, Monroe, and Madison would have none of that. They concentrated on expansion whatever the consequences to the principle of self-determination. After Jefferson acquired Louisiana in 1803, for example, he was callous and condescending toward its French and Spanish inhabitants. "They are as yet incapable of self-government as children." [5] Thomas Paine, that dynamic spokesman for the unique American Present, wholly agreed. "We have a right to the possession," echoed the New York *Evening Post*. "The interests of the human race demand from us exertion of this right." America even then considered itself destined to self-determine the world.

The preferences of the citizens of Louisiana were ignored. Jefferson sent troops to enforce his decision that they were laggards from the Past unprepared for the good American Present. He decreed that they should be neither citizens of a state or a territory—and gave them no representation. He chose their leaders. The critical petitions of the time called it "inconsistent with every principle of civil liberty," and even Jefferson's kindly biographer calls it "unmis-

[5] L. W. Levy, *Jefferson and Civil Liberties, The Darker Side* (Cambridge, Harvard University Press, 1963) pp. 81–92.

takably despotic." Jefferson had his ready defense. Those people, he told Gallatin, were not "ripe" for the American Present.

John Quincy Adams, who wanted the continent as a young woman wants a man, voted for the Louisiana Purchase and then attacked Jefferson on the issues of self-determination and self-government. He was supported by an equally bold congressman from Tennessee who called Jefferson's plan "a system of tyranny." [6] Jefferson ignored them all. The rhetoric of self-determination had been recruited to the cause of preserving the Present. Other Latin Americans were to learn the same lesson.

[6] While I have investigated many primary sources in the preparation of this chapter, I happily acknowledge the articles and books researched and written by the following people. They were unusually helpful. H. Blumenthal, H. Dupre, C. D. Hazen, B. F. Hyslop, C. L. R. James, L. S. Kaplan, R. L. Ketcham, R. W. Logan, D. Malone, L. L. Montague, G. de B. de Sauvigny, L. M. Sears, J. I. Shulim, T. L. Stoddard, and E. B. White.

# 3

# The Vision of
# an American System
# to Preserve the Present

[Our system] will fit a larger empire than ever yet
existed, and I have long believed that such an empire
will rise in America, and give quiet to the world.
                              —Matthew Lyon, Representative from
                                    Vermont and Kentucky, 1816

It is in our power to create a system of which we shall
be the center and in which all South America
will act with us.
                                                —Henry Clay, 1820

America goes not abroad in search of monsters
to destroy. . . . She might become the dictatress of
the world; she would no longer be the ruler of
her own spirit.
                                      —John Quincy Adams, 1821

The political system of the [European] powers is
essentially different . . . from that of America. . . .
We owe it, therefore in candor . . . to declare that we

should consider any attempt on their part to extend
their system to any portion of this hemisphere as
dangerous to our peace and safety.

—President James Monroe, 1823

We are running wild about the Greeks.

—Joel Roberts Poinsett, Special Agent
to Latin America and Representative
from South Carolina, 1823

Americans concluded that the French Revolution was
a failure that nevertheless posed worrisome problems. First,
by not creating another America, the French had left the
United States still isolated—surrounded by the Bad Past.
Second, they had offered two dangerous examples: a radicalism that threatened the idea of liberty developed in the
United States, and an idealism that was so broad as to question the uniqueness and the mission of America. A perceptive historian caught the essence of such conservatism in a
few thoughtful words. Americans were disgusted with it all
because they felt that those who failed to emulate the United
States "had proved unworthy of the confidence that had
been placed in them." [1]

Hence it was a joy to turn away from France and
embrace the South Americans who were fighting for independence from Europe. And a duty to encourage them—at
least to the degree that their conception of independence
promised to end the isolation of the United States, to enlarge
its commerce, and to lead them to fall into place as junior
members of an American system that would preserve the
Present.

[1] Edward Howard Tatum, Jr., *The United States and Europe, 1815–1823*
(New York, Russell & Russell, 1936), p. 39.

# I

It was hardly surprising that Henry Clay of Kentucky took the lead in advocating a policy of recognizing their right of self-determination and integrating them into a system dominated by the United States. Clay was a charismatic leader who probably exercised more power and influence than any other early nineteenth-century politician who failed to be elected President—and more than several who did make it to the White House. He burst upon the national scene in 1811 as a dynamic leader determined to launch a second war against Great Britain, and he concluded his career arranging a compromise to prevent a revolution in the United States.

Many years ago (during the 1920s and the 1930s) there was a popular cartoon that offered illuminating insights into social history under the flexible title of "Born Thirty Years Too Soon" or "Born Thirty Years Too Late," and Clay would have offered a perfect subject. He should have been a Founding Father or a leader during a much later period. He was fired by a commitment to self-determination and at the same time understood the need to limit that right through compromise in order to build a community. He argued passionately (and effectively) for war to prevent America from being recolonized by Britain's burgeoning economic power (and to acquire more territory), and he called with equal insistence (but no success) for Americans to surrender some of their individual freedom to create a national political economy.

The revolt of the Spanish colonies, which was triggered by the Napoleonic Wars, prompted Clay to extend that vision to the Western Hemisphere. He turned from the second war for independence against England (1812–15) to that struggle without missing a step. Driven by a mighty conviction of America's uniqueness and mission (as well as a deep sense of the necessity to expand), he exulted in the confidence that "we are too powerful for the mightiest nation in Europe or all Europe united."

He considered his proposal to create an American system by recognizing and supporting the Latin American revolutionaries to be the most momentous foreign policy question which he could "conceive of as ever arising": it concerned "our politics, our commerce, our navigation." "It is in our power to create a system of which we shall be the center and in which all South America will act with us." To fail to seize the opportunity would be to "pass sentence of condemnation upon the founders of our liberty."[2]

Clay no more stood alone in his campaign to create a hemispheric system than he had been a solitary advocate of integrating mission, self-determination, and expansion in another war against Great Britain. Representative David Trimble of Kentucky offered a broad historical analysis in 1818 based on the apocalyptic proposition that "we see the beginning, not the end of revolutions. . . . We live in the crisis of all ages. . . . A great moral crisis—a great commercial crisis." The bad old European system could be toppled, and hence it was the responsibility of the United States to "feed the famished nations with the food of independence"; and to fulfill that mission it needed to create a "great system" in the Western Hemisphere. "Heaven, in giving freedom to us first, made it our primal eldest duty."

[2] Anyone who explores the ensuing debate about this vision of an American system must begin with Charles C. Griffin, *The United States and the Disruption of the Spanish Empire, 1810–1822* (New York, Octagon, 1937); and Arthur P. Whitaker, *The United States and the Independence of Latin America, 1800–1830* (New York, W. W. Norton, 1941). But Mitzi Mahaffey caught many revealing congressional comments, and sensed some subtle nuances that escaped even those scholars.

Another congressman, Thomas B. Robertson of Louisiana, anticipated the "direct pecuniary advantages" that would flow from recognizing and supporting the revolutions, but also displayed a keen desire to end America's isolation. "I do hope," he declared in 1818, "we are not the sole depository of all that survives, the ark that floats alone on the universal deluge." To act boldly will "give us confidence." The head of the Patent Office, William Thornton, pushed economic arguments but also drafted a model constitution and outlined other reforms to help bring the Past into the Present.

The concern to expand American commerce was very strong among many groups. Jefferson had revealed that pressure as early as 1786, when he expressed the hope that circumstances would enable the United States to self-determine the Spanish territories "piece by piece" into an American system. A typical supporter of Clay viewed Latin America as the key to the *future prosperity, commerce, and security* of the United States. And Matthew Lyon of Kentucky wrote to James Monroe, an ardent missionary in the cause of American republicanism who was just about to become President, that the principles underpinning the United States would "fit a larger empire than ever yet existed." He had "long believed that such an empire will arise in America and give quiet to the world." It was time to begin that process by "Anglo-Americanizing" the hemisphere.

## II

Not everyone agreed, however, with those who thought that events in Latin America presented a "sublime spectacle." Many southerners, along with some northerners, were uneasy about colored people making revolutions against established authority. Others had been disillusioned by events in Paris. The Latins "will taste the cup of liberty and will like the French become inebriated with its contents, and like the French will wade through scenes of blood and horrors." The editors of many publications, ranging from *Niles' Register* through the *National Gazette* to the *North American Review*, shared similar fears. Others attacked the idea that the United States was somehow "the Guarantor of the Liberties of the World." No one has appointed us, thundered John Quincy Adams, as judges of "the righteous cause."

It was difficult to challenge Adams. His credentials were too impeccable and his performances were too impressive. He was an expansionist committed to continental empire, and yet a man who respected and tried to honor the commitment to the principle of self-determination. He bluntly and effectively argued the wisdom of not recognizing the Latin Americans until Spain had agreed to a territorial settlement west of the Mississippi that would give the United States a pathway to the Pacific. Having negotiated that treaty (signed in February, 1819), he went to the heart of the matter about the South American revolutions.

He supported their struggle for self-determination and thought the resulting commercial benefits to the United States might prove significant; but he vigorously opposed the kind of activist policy advocated by Clay and others. Displaying some racial prejudice, along with considerable realism, Adams argued that the cultures and political traditions of Latin America were so different, and the economic conditions so dissimilar that it was nonsense to talk about an American System. He was supported by others, like Joel Roberts Poinsett, who had investigated the situation in South America.

Adams was even more disturbed by the interventionism inherent in Clay's approach, and the psychological momentum being generated in support of a jingoistic and adventuristic foreign policy. He confided to a friend that the propensity to crusade was the "most pernicious tendency" among Americans; and warned that indulging that penchant would "change the very foundations of our own government from *liberty* to *power*."

And so John Quincy Adams made a dramatic speech. A Fourth of July Oration in 1821 to explain how to keep America free. The United States, he began, was unique: it had "swept away all the rubbish of accumulated centuries of servitude." And it did have a mission: to develop that uniqueness in science, literature, and the arts as an example of what human beings could accomplish. But it all would be lost if the United States undertook a campaign to save the world.

"America goes not abroad in search of monsters to destroy. . . . She well knows that by once enlisting under ✓ other banners than her own, were they even the banners of foreign independence, she would involve herself, beyond the power of extrication, in all the wars of interest and intrigue, of individual avarice, envy, and ambition, which assume the colors and usurp the standard of freedom. . . . She might become the dictatress of the world; she would no longer be the ruler of her own spirit."

Adams was exceptional, but he was also ordinary in his inability to act immediately on all of his insights into the truth. Hence he agreed with Clay and others on the special virtue of the American Present and played a crucial part in asserting the right of the United States to prevent Europeans from reintroducing the Bad Past into the Western Hemisphere.

That major diplomatic maneuver began early in 1822, when President Monroe recommended the recognition of the revolutionary governments in Chile, Colombia, Mexico, and Argentina. The Spanish government then in power had, with understandable reluctance, accepted the loss of the empire. But those leaders were shortly overturned by a French invasion which restored Ferdinand VII to the throne. The mind of the Spanish monarch was atumble with revengeful schemes, and it was soon reported that he was planning to reconquer Spanish America with the aid of France and Russia,. and perhaps Austria and Prussia.

Those rumors rekindled the earlier American anger against Russia. The Czar had taken the lead in 1815 to create an alignment of conservative and reactionary governments, known as the Holy Alliance, designed to prevent further upheavals like the French Revolution—or to repress them if they did occur. Clay played upon those emotions to sustain his campaign, and others like President Monroe grew alarmed or discouraged.

Those leaders were inclined to accept England's proposal to join in making a strong declaration against any attempt to restore Spanish power in the Western Hemisphere. The British had played a major part in suppressing the French Revolution but had become concerned about the willingness of its allies to use force in ways that threatened its own interests—including expanded trade with South America. Adams was more perceptive than most other Americans, however, and realized that England's opposition made it very unlikely that France or any other power would undertake the kind of massive campaign required to reconquer Spanish America.

Hence he viewed the situation as being full of opportunities rather than being clogged with problems. The United States could step forward as the champion of the principle of self-determination and at the same time make it clear that it would not allow the Good American Present to be subverted by the Bad Past. That strategy also offered a way to outflank Clay in the fight to succeed Monroe as President.

Adams won the argument within the Cabinet, and on December 2, 1823, Monroe announced to the world the birth of an American System headed by the United States. It was time to assert, "as a principle in which the rights and interests of the United States are involved, that the American continents, by the free and independent condition which they have assumed and maintain, are henceforth not to be considered as subjects for future colonization by any European powers.

"The political system of the allied powers is essentially different . . . from that of America. . . . We owe it, therefore, to candor and to the amicable relations existing between the United States and those powers to declare that we should consider any attempt on their part to extend their system to any portion of this hemisphere as dangerous to our peace and safety. . . . It is impossible that the allied powers should extend their political system to any portion of either continent without endangering our peace and happiness."

Those were bold and revealing words. They did not prevent the Holy Alliance from invading Latin America, for that idea never had much substance, but they did self-determine the Western Hemisphere as an American System within which the United States was the dominant power. The struggle over how that predominance would be used, personified by the initial clash between Clay and Adams, continued on into the twentieth century.[3]

---

[3] A preview was provided by Clay. Despite all his rhetoric about the right of the South Americans to self-determine themselves he was vehemently opposed to any revolutionary activity in Cuba. That was to be controlled by the United States and hence must be made secure from "all ideas of independence."

## III

So, also, did the related dispute about the ultimate *size* of the American System. That issue had been raised as an integral part of the debate about Latin America. For that matter, President Monroe almost perfectly revealed the interaction between the two issues in the course of his remarks about the system. He began with the Western Hemisphere, then offered "most ardent wishes" for the success of the Greek revolutionaries, and then returned to the discussion of Latin America.

There had been rallies and other expressions of support for the Greek struggle against Turkey before that time, but, together with Edward Everett's militant article in *The North Atlantic Review*, Monroe's comments of December, 1823, generated a fresh outburst of enthusiasm.[4] By the end of the month, as one astute politician observed, the country was "running wild about the Greeks." Representative Daniel Webster of Massachusetts then introduced a resolution in January, 1824, that focused the commotion.

Praising the Greeks for their courage "in the cause of liberty and Christianity," he called for action to support them in keeping with our "sense of our own duty, our character, and our interest." The ensuing discussion revealed three interests: expanded commerce; the Christian American mission to reform the world; and a desire to establish a beachhead of the American Present in the European Past. One or all of those objectives moved people from New York to

---

[4] The two most useful studies are Myrtle A. Cline, *American Attitudes Toward the Greek War of Independence, 1821–1828* (Atlanta, n.p., 1930); and Stephen A. Larrabee, *Hellas Observed. The American Experience of Greece, 1775–1865* (New York, New York U. Press, 1957). Again, however, I am indebted to Mitzi Mahaffey: her keen eye for neglected information and her perceptions into what it means. Everett was a distinguished New England intellectual who was also a political activist.

Louisiana, and from South Carolina to the Mississippi, to demand intervention.

Webster and Clay wanted to send an American agent to establish commercial ties with the Greeks and also to provide moral support. Others agitated to send the navy. Many petitioners stressed the obligation to help fellow Christians and the opportunity to punish the barbarous Turks. And still another group emphasized the chance to weaken the Holy Alliance and provoke more revolutions.

The opposition used the same arguments in rebuttal. It was not only grossly hypocritical to denounce intervention in the Western Hemisphere while undertaking it in Europe, they pointed out, but also the height of irresponsibility to risk inciting a general war. That would lose more commerce than could ever be gained with Greece and might well lead to the recolonization of South America. It could even threaten the existence of the United States—"the best hope of the rest of the world."

Clay appealed to that sense of uniqueness in trying to shame his opponents into action: "are we so humbled, so low, so debased . . . so mean, so base, so despicable that we may not attempt to express our horror?" But he was beaten back by those who answered that *he* was the one who lacked faith in the power of America as an example. The American Present could be sustained and ultimately enlarged without embarking upon an intervention that "could only be regarded in the light of a crusade."

The missionary activists who sought to help other people self-determine their Past into the American Present remained vocal and influential despite their defeat over Greece. Their persistence began, moreover, to raise among many Americans the question of whether the principle of self-determination was going to be applied in that fashion *within* America.

# 4

# Omens of a
# Bloody Determination
# to Preserve the Present

There ariseth a little cloud out of the sea, like a man's
hand.

—I Kings. 18:44

We have the wolf by the ears, and we can neither safely
hold him, nor safely let him go.

—Thomas Jefferson, 1820

The race of Indians will perish! Yes, sir!
—Congressman Richard Henry Wilde of Georgia, 1823

The very idea of an *American People,* as constituting a
single community, is a mere chimera. Such a
community never, for a single moment, existed,—
neither before nor since the Declaration of
Independence.

—John Caldwell Calhoun, 1831

But the game is caught; and I believe it is true, that
with the catching, end the pleasures of the chase. This
field of glory is harvested, and the crop is already

appropriated. But new reapers will arise, and *they*,
too, will seek a field. . . . Towering genius disdains a
beaten path. . . . It scorns to tread in the footsteps
of *any* predecessor, however illustrious. It thirsts and
burns for distinction; and, if possible, it will have it,
whether at the expense of emancipating slaves,
or enslaving men.

—Abraham Lincoln, 1838

The uneasiness about crusades to preserve the Present,
and the related realization that the right of self-determination cut two ways, that became apparent during the debates
about the revolutions in Latin America and Greece, were
intimately connected with development *within* America.
John Quincy Adams was not alone in warning about the
dangers of such militant philanthropy. His inveterate political enemy John Randolph shared those fears. Such a campaign, he warned, "gathers power in the going." "Sir," he
cried, "the sun never sets on ambition like this: they who
have once felt its scorpion sting are never satisfied with a
limit less than a circle of our planet."

The House of Representatives Committee on Foreign
Affairs cut down to the bone. "Even when civil war breaks
the bonds of society and government, it gives birth in the
nation to two independent parties. . . . It is of necessity,
therefore, that these two parties should be considered by
foreign states as two distinct and independent nations. To
consider or treat them otherwise, would be to interfere in
their domestic concerns, to deny them the right to manage
their own affairs in their own way, and to violate the essential attributes of their respective sovereignty." [1]

The visceral issues of independence, sovereignty, and
separation into two or more confederations had always been

[1] Report of March 19, 1822.

close to the center of the American dialogue. They were periodically mooted by conflicts with England and other foreign
nations (including the First Americans), or sublimated in
the desire and determination to expand, and to reform the
world, but they persistently reasserted their primacy. It was
from the beginning a question of whose Present was going
to predominate.

## I

The colonies finally agreed, as they performed their
separate minuets up to the brink of revolution, that there
would be no ball unless they danced together. But John
Adams illustrated the localism of all in his remark that Massachusetts was "our country." Each colony was different, and
highly self-conscious of its peculiar virtues and institutions,
and the idea of Union was initially viewed far more as a
means of preserving distinctiveness than as an end defined
by one community.

New Englanders and southerners knew and treasured
their respective Presents, and they wanted to preserve them
in pristine form. Bostonians considered southerners backward—dullards slow to recognize the value of the modern
world. As for Pennsylvania, its females, livestock, and grains
were less desirable, less tasty, and less nourishing. Their
morals were likewise more licentious and their manners
boorish. They were in truth inferior.

Southerners joyfully reciprocated. New Englanders
were hypocrites who preached democracy for everyone else
while perfecting an aristocracy that ruled the political economy through the manipulation of the rhetoric of equality.
Taxation on the basis of population was nothing more than
an extra petticoat effected to hide the value of northern land.
Slavery was one labor system; the irresponsible, indifferent,

and often inhumane practice of paying the lowest possible wage in the marketplace was simply another way of extracting profits. You take your present, I'll take mine. I'll honor your self-determination, you honor mine.[2]

The Articles of Confederation recognized and sought to respect those differences while providing for the essential commonalities. But that imaginative and potentially creative approach to self-government failed because it was in truth a leap into the Future. The colonists remained the children of mercantilism. Isolated in relative weakness outside the British Empire, driven by their sense of unique mission, and convinced of the necessity of expansion, they compromised their self-determination in the name of empire. The Constitution proved more suited to preserving the Present.

# II

But the other vision could not be wiped from the mind. John Taylor of Caroline Country, Virginia, seriously discussed separation with Rufus King and Oliver Ellsworth of New England in 1794, and much of the opposition to the Louisiana Purchase turned upon a concern about the primary value of self-determination and the northern desire to preserve its own Present. Madison's argument that empire would enable everyone to enjoy his own version of the truth carried the day, just as it had opened the way for the adoption of the Constitution. With enough Hail Marys to such a Holy Grail, almost anything could be justified. Even another war against Great Britain that Madison called a struggle to prevent the recolonization of the American political

[2] On these attitudes, and the early talk of separation, see H. von Holst, *The Constitutional and Political History of the United States*, Vol. I (New York, AMS Press, 1872); Merrill Jensen, *The Articles of Confederation* (1940); and Charles S. Syndor, *The Development of Southern Sectionalism, 1819–1948* (Baton Rouge, Louisiana State U. Press, 1948).

economy. A second war for independence, republican purity, and empire—all in the name of the mission to reform the world (including the Floridas and Canada).

Jefferson had long before stopped even talking about a continent of loosely associated commonwealths. He sustained the spirit of imperial independence and self-determination through a war against the Barbary States; his secret explanation of the imperial purposes of the Lewis and Clark expedition; his irrational vendetta against Aaron Burr (who dared to act on Jefferson's earlier words about separate republics), and his attempts to bring the belligerents of the Napoleonic Wars to terms devised in America. They were all maneuvers to sustain the American Present.

All to no lasting success. It was probably true that New Englanders like Ellsworth misread Taylor's further remarks about separation—he was not then ready for firm action—but they were close to the mark in commenting that the North and the South "never had and never would think alike." Taylor soon wanted a showdown and gave way only under strong pressure from Jefferson. But within five years he was resigned to the inevitable necessity of invoking the right of self-determination to preserve the South's Present. "I give up all for lost," Taylor said. He openly despised commercial and industrial capitalism, and candidly defended slavery on the grounds that it was better to be controlled by another human being than dominated by the impersonal abstractions of a class or the marketplace.

Northerners who defined the Present rather narrowly as commercial capitalism fondled the idea of secession during the second war for independence. No one knows precisely how close they came to acting on that possibility during the discussions that preceded their 1814 meeting in Hartford, Connecticut, or during the debates of that convention to protest the war. But their activities served to maintain and widen that path for others to follow. "There is no magic in the sound of Union," thundered Pickering. "If the great objects of union are utterly abandoned . . . let the Union be dissolved." Identical sentiments were shortly reiterated by southerners who cited Hartford as the precedent for their own activities.

Those developments grew out of the War of 1812. While that conflict ostensibly ended in a stalemate, it proved in truth to be a subtle victory for the United States. England's hard-earned sense of history enabled it to put first things first: to recognize that reconquering all or part of the United States would be a bloody irrelevancy—a detour into the Past when victory over Napoleon opened a glorious vista into the Future. The meaning of that decision for America was simple: it could (and did) push Spain to the wall to extract a vast vista to the Pacific. John Quincy Adams managed the strategy and the negotiations in masterful style.

# III

It appeared grand, but shortly turned miserable. For, even as Adams secured a base to control the continent (and a toehold for a leap into Asia), he confronted the question of whether or not slavery would be allowed to share that victory. If one said *no*, then one faced secession at a time when America needed all its strength to preserve the Present and sustain its mission. The vision of an American System would disappear even before it was fully formulated. But if one said *yes*, then one faced the prospect of compromising the mission in order to fulfill the mission. Adams ultimately recognized that it was necessary either to say *no* to missionary expansion or to accept the corruption of the mission as the price of expansion. But in 1820 he compromised on the basis of another grand vision.

Like Washington and others, Adams understood that the only possible way to sustain republicanism in a continental setting was somehow to create a continental community. Otherwise, and probably sooner than anyone expected, the society would fragment into several different political economies that could be controlled only through increasing centralization and coercion. Even Madison ultimately admitted the power of that logic and anticipated that the republic would someday become a monarchy.

The record of the developing thought of those men leaves the observer with a powerful, if somewhat intangible, feeling that they were wrestling with a growing awareness that Madison's theory was wrong. And of course he was wrong. For in grounding democratic republican government in expansion, there is no recourse but to move from the Atlantic to the Mississippi to the Pacific to the world to the universe. If excess social space and a surplus of resources are deemed essential, then expansion becomes a categorical imperative. Yet the more the expansion the less the democracy, for an empire cannot be governed as a republic. The forms may survive, but the substance withers.

There is in the end, therefore, no recourse but to honor the right of self-determination of other groups, including those who choose to break away from the empire. That means accepting the Past and acknowledging that the Present will give way to a different Future. Adams ultimately recognized that truth, but in the meantime he developed a two-pronged strategy for resolving the dilemma without abandoning the imperial base for the Present. One proposal involved setting a limit on expansion: explicit control of the continent, from Canada to the Gulf of Mexico, and from the Atlantic to the Pacific, would enable the United States to dominate the Western Hemisphere, and that power base would underwrite a global commerce that would not require political empire. The other plan called for developing the continental republic as one balanced political economy grounded in the integration of agriculture, finance, manufacturing, and commerce. That meant national planning to create a system of internal improvements, and education, that would in turn generate a shared life and culture.

Washington had earlier devised a similar approach. He realized that the topography of the eastern slope of the continent perpetuated and exacerbated the social differences between the North and the South. People north of Chesapeake Bay went west along different routes than those who lived south of Baltimore, and the result was a further weakening of community. The back country was being settled in a way that intensified the differences of the two peoples. He proposed to drive a national highway westward through the mountains from Baltimore and Washington. That would not only bring northerners and southerners together as they went west, but it would develop the Chesapeake area as the great center of a mixed economy. And that, he felt, would provide the basis—through jobs and the diffusion of population—for the gradual demise of slavery.

It was a powerful conception, and just might have worked as he hoped—at least for the eastern half of the continent. After he became Secretary of the Treasury in 1801, Albert Gallatin ultimately translated the vision into a mind-boggling Ten-Year Plan for a system of internal improvements designed to provide the physical basis for a national community. Whatever chance it had to be realized, however, was irrevocably undermined by the crisis over the extension of slavery into Missouri. Adams recognized all the ramifications of that confrontation at least as clearly as Jefferson did, and even fondled the surgeon's knife of separation into two nations.

Both men viewed it as one of those blood-red sun-

WILLIAM APPLEMAN WILLIAMS

rises that old sailors read as an omen of terrible times. Jefferson argued that the act of drawing a line on the continent to separate slave agriculture from the rest of the country would inevitably mean the end of America—the end of the Present, the end of uniqueness, and the end of the mission. He used two striking metaphors to express his sense of doom.

The one most often quoted is indeed electric. "This momentous question, like a fire bell in the night, awakened and filled me with terror. I considered it at once as the Knell of the Union." The other is no less striking, and perhaps more perceptive. "We have the wolf by the ears, and we can neither safely hold him, nor safely let him go." He sensed that few had the nerve to risk the Future.

Adams was one of those. He considered letting go. His familiarity with the early discussions of separation, including the one caused by the acquisition of Louisiana, led him to confront the issue directly. "I love the Union as I love my wife," he wrote in 1801. "But if my wife should ask and insist upon a separation, she should have it, though it broke my heart." A desperately painful choice, but Adams faced it once again during the Missouri Crisis. Slavery was "precisely the question" upon which to dissolve the Union; and perhaps it was the catalytic moment to reorganize the nonslave states through a new constitutional convention. That action might well persuade the southerners to accept gradual emancipation.

But Adams never rang that fire bell. The question of why is forever tantalizing, and so is the answer. Even Adams did not bare that much of himself in the almost endless pages of his diary and other writings. He surely knew that he would be challenging the Present that his fellow citizens valued so highly, and that most of them cared little for the Black Americans. And division would risk the fulfillment of the mission to which he was as committed as the next person.

He was also ambitious. Not merely to be President, but even more powerfully driven to solve the problem—to purify and sustain the Present as part of fulfilling the uniqueness and the mission. That, indeed, was the Adams mission. Therein, most probably, lies the answer to the question.

In any event, more southerners than northerners emerged from the confrontation thinking about the possibility of secession. They viewed themselves ever more on the defensive, and more than a few talked portentously of acting on the right of self-determination. "We shall ere long be compelled to calculate the value of our Union," predicted Thomas Cooper of South Carolina in 1827, "and to enquire of what use to us is this most unequal alliance." Those were the whispers from the portico that most northerners chose to ignore.

## IV

The Present proved its worth, moreover, in dealing with the immediate question of acquiring more land. At the cost, however, of eroding the cornerstone of the right of self-determination. Put bluntly, as it should be, northerners and southerners joined hands to destroy the independence and meaningful existence of the First Americans.[3] Having initially viewed them as prior and equal societies to be dealt with in classic treaty relationships, most white Americans rapidly redefined the Red People as part of the Past that had either to be forced into the Present or destroyed.

In one important respect, of course, surrounding the First Americans with the evolving marketplace capitalism of

[3] I prefer, as more accurate and respectful, the terms *First Americans* and *Red People,* over the traditional nomenclature of *Indian,* for collective references to the various societies that existed in the Western Hemisphere prior to the arrival of Europeans.

the 1820s and 1830s was a subtle technique of destruction. But one of the basic characteristics of a viable culture is its ability to adapt to changing circumstances, and many First Americans displayed that capacity whenever they were offered the slightest opportunity. Given a reasonable and equitable economic foundation, for example, many hunting and quasinomadic groups proved that they could use the environment at least as well as those who installed European systems. And others, particularly in the South, demonstrated an enviable talent for sustaining the essence of their way of life while shifting to the white man's kind of agriculture. Impressive people. Their destruction previewed the shift by white Americans from a commitment to the right of revolutionary self-determination to the practice of counterrevolution to preserve the Present.

The displacement and the killing of the First Americans began almost immediately, but it did not become a matter of coordinated *policy* until the early nineteenth century. Jonathan Edwards and John Eliot were by no means the only white men who sought a way of living with the Red People. Indeed, if there had been a clear and firm policy in those early years it might have issued in a workable compromise. For that matter, the treaty approach bespoke a basic kind of respect and esteem.

That policy was carried forward by men like Adams, Madison, and Monroe. It was impossible, even for southerners used to slavery, not to acknowledge the grandeur of the First Americans. "I think they are a noble, gallant, injured race," remarked Virginia Congressman Thomas Bouldin. "I think they have suffered nothing but wrong and injury from us." They tended to die under slavery—or accept death in flight as a better fate. The early decimation was more the result of the implacable logic of the fur trade (a nasty busi-

80

ness in any light), and every European's desire to enter and preserve the unique American Present, than any calculated assault upon their integrity and existence. And in 1820 there were at least 125,000 First Americans still alive and functioning east of the Mississippi.

It was southerners like Madison, for that matter, who promised the First Americans that they would be dealt with as equals as they accepted the essentials of the white Present. Settle down and cultivate the soil, and you will be left alone. It was not a generous, not even a truly equitable, proposal; but it did offer a meaningful basis for cohabitation of the continent. But for people who believed that the Present in all its essentials depended upon expansion, even that potentially workable compromise proved intolerable. The Past was a threat, and the First Americans who became successful farmers were not at all abstract. They were there on the land, doing very well indeed, thank you.

A troublesome matter. They could be called children, but they functioned as adults. They could be called barbarians, but they displayed an uncanny and unnerving sophistication. All that aside, white Americans needed the land to preserve their way of life. For without the land the Present would inevitably slide into the Past. And so began the massive campaign against their right of self-determination. From being treated as equals dealt with through treaties, they became wards to be ruled with benevolence and educated (and otherwise induced) to accept the American Present.

Or killed.

A superficial view lays the new approach in the lap of the southerners. That is history written by the North, which ultimately asserted its definition of the Present. But the North was only doing to the South what it had done earlier to the Red People. Northerners pushed the First

Americans into limbo as part of the wars against the British and the French which were defined as national necessities. The last courageous stand by the Sacs in the Black Hawk War of 1832 was overridden without any serious debate in the Congress—or elsewhere.

Adams and Monroe did insist, as long as they had any power, that removal across the Mississippi could proceed only with the consent of the Red People. That momentarily saved some 50,000 Cherokees, Creeks, Choctaws, Chickasaws, and Seminoles who occupied about 33 million acres in the South. But it was mostly good land for short staple cotton, with other profits in the clearing, and one did not have to own slaves to recognize its value for preserving the American way. Hence it was by no means only the speculators and the big planters who called the turn. Everyman wanted his share.

The Cherokees in Georgia had taken Madison at his word. They established a state within a state—and made it work. Georgia whites took them to court. Twice. And both times the judges honored the early treaties. So Georgia waited for Andrew Jackson to replace Adams and then moved to deny the self-determination of the Cherokees. Jackson talked much of independence, honor, and self-determination, but he meant it first for himself and then for other whites who accepted his leadership. The First Americans were uprooted and forced westward to their doom. Thousands were killed in the process, but the American way of life was secured.

# V

Georgia's strategy for destroying the First Americans was quickly copied by Alabama and Mississippi. And its

82

related technique of quarantining free Black sailors on ships that visited its ports was shortly used by South Carolina. The concern about slavery that was revealed in those prohibitions had grown steadily after the Missouri Crisis. The expansion of short staple cotton acreage was only part of the explanation for the rising tension over the issue. Black militance was a vital factor. The aborted rising planned by Denmark Vesey in 1822 led to repressive measures in many states, and David Walker's brilliant and radical attack on slavery in 1829, *Appeal to the Colored Citizens of the World*, further increased the alarm.

The upsurge in white abolitionism, in part triggered by the religious revivalism of the late 1820s, and which culminated in the launching of the fiery *Liberator* edited by William Lloyd Garrison, likewise intensified southern fears. Perhaps even more disturbing was the growing sentiment in Virginia for gradual emancipation. That dramatized the issue at least as forcefully as abolitionist rhetoric.

All those developments occurred, moreover, as southerners were becoming ever more upset about their economic and political power in relation to the North. It was the classic confrontation between the city and the country that Adam Smith described so candidly and starkly in *The Wealth of Nations;* and the South viewed its experience as verifying his judgment that the city enjoyed an inherent and devastating advantage. "Wealth will be transferred to the North," warned Thomas Cooper of South Carolina in 1827, "and wealth is power. . . . We shall, before long, be compelled to calculate the value of our union; and to enquire of what use to us is this most unequal alliance?"

Others expressed themselves more bluntly. The South was carrying the North on its back, and hence the criticism of slavery was moralistic cant. If the North wanted to leave, let it go. When a man tried to talk about the issues, one complained in disgust with "the ultimate tendency of the 'System'" to impoverish the South. "They stun you with all the slamwhangery of fourth of July patriotism, the greatness of the Union and the blood and thunder of civil war."

Those attitudes and feelings created a highly volatile mixture, and the passage in 1828 of an extremely high tariff bill that favored northern interests touched off an explosion that mushroomed into a major crisis involving slavery and secession. Much of the initial commotion was caused by incendiaries like Cooper, James Hamilton, Jr., Robert Barnwell Rhett, and Robert Y. Hayne, but John Caldwell Calhoun rapidly became the central figure in the confrontation with the North. Calhoun was in some respects the southern equivalent of John Quincy Adams: an austere loner of great intelligence who concentrated his awesome energies on major issues. He very quickly placed the right of self-determination at the center of the debate about America.

Calhoun initially sought to realize the vision of a continental community; using his powers as Secretary of War, for example, to begin constructing a system of internal improvements. His shift to the position of southern sectionalist was no doubt influenced by the political necessities in South Carolina, and by his own ambitions, but it is a mistake to discount a less mundane motive.

He correctly perceived that the rise of Andrew Jackson symbolized the end of the effort to create a national community. The age of the Founding Fathers died in 1824, a victim of the mangled election of John Quincy Adams. The subsequent triumph of Jackson in 1828 redefined the central political problem as one of devising a way to honor and institutionalize the principle of self-determination within an American empire that was increasingly taking on the forms and practices of marketplace capitalism. Calhoun was immediately concerned about the South simply because he was a South Carolinian, but his approach was applicable to any similar region.[4] His solution to the problem was ultimately formalized as the theory of the concurrent majority, but its essentials emerged clearly during the crisis of 1828–32.

Calhoun began with an attack on the tariff of 1828 as "unconstitutional, unequal, and oppressive." It reduced southerners (but also other farmers) to "the serfs of the system" who paid a huge tax to enrich northerners. Then he outlined the options. "If there be no protective power in the reserved rights of the states, they must in the end be forced to rebel, or submit to have their permanent interests sacrificed, their domestick institutions subverted by Colonization and other schemes and themselves and children reduced to wretchedness."

The argument of course involved a defense of slavery, but it was a defense grounded in the fundamental right of any people to go to Hell in their own way. Slavery is evil. But Calhoun was arguing that the revolutionary right of self-determination denies one culture the right to impose its Heaven upon another. He thus defined the issue in the starkest possible terms. Either honor the principle, or embrace the imperial ethic of forcing others to do what you want them to do or do what you think they should do. He likewise clarified the inherent tension between America's commitment to self-determination, its sense of unique mission to reform the world, and its belief in the necessity and desirability of expansion.

The South Carolina legislature shortly adopted resolutions against the tariff and was supported by Georgia, Mississippi, and Virginia. Hayne then carried the issue into the

---

[4] Calhoun was also deeply concerned with maintaining upper-class rule and saw his evolving ideas as a means to that end (for northerners as well as southerners), but that is not the focus of this essay.

Senate during his famous 1830 debates with Daniel Webster.[5] Sovereignty, cried Hayne, is not subject to adjudication in the courts. The right of self-determination is inviolable. Jackson accepted the challenge, and in a famous confrontation with Calhoun asserted the primacy of the national government. "Our Union: it must be preserved." "The Union," Calhoun shot back, "next to our liberty, most dear. May we always remember that it can only be preserved by distributing equally the benefits and burdens of the Union."

There the matter seemed to rest, but it was in truth fermenting within the hothouse of another crisis. Virginia legislators revealed serious divisions over how to deal with the institution of slavery during those same months, and Nat Turner's bloody slave uprising of August, 1831, provoked (along with a massacre of Blacks) a visceral debate about emancipation. Young westerners favored ending slavery on moral and pragmatic grounds, and economic difficulties of the state led some eastern planters to join them.

But the economic troubles also underscored the difficulty of absorbing free Blacks. The problems inherent in that fundamental social change loomed even more formidably in the context of unemployment. And the first issue of Garrison's *Liberator,* which appeared in the midst of the debate with a bellicose cry for immediate abolition, underscored the intense fears generated by Turner's insurrection. Though the votes on some of the proposals dealing with emancipation were close, thus posing an eternal enigma about the consequences of Turner's action,[6] the final de-

---

[5] This confrontation began over the issue of public land policy, another question that divided the city and the country, but quickly became a sharp exchange focused on the right of self-determination.

[6] Though not, of course, about the right or justification for such action. The enigma is an inherent part of radical (or conservative) violence, and involves the tension between being driven to act *no matter what* and choosing the most consequential moment. It is not a question of criticizing Turner, but rather a matter of reflecting upon, and learning from, his particular decision.

cision favored slavery. That touched off a general movement throughout the South to extend the existing controls over slaves and led in many states to laws forbidding emancipation.

Two months after Turner's assault, Governor Hamilton of South Carolina moved to implement the 1828 decision to oppose the tariff. The result was a convention that, on November 24, 1831, passed various measures designed to nullify the law in that state. It also declared that the use of force by the national government would justify secession and authorized the organization of a military force. Jackson was furious. He called the action "treason," spouted fire about "the wickedness, madness, and folly of the leaders [and] the delusion of their followers," alerted government forces, and demanded congressional approval for marching an army into South Carolina.

The President also used his charisma and political clout to arrange a compromise on the tariff. Calhoun proposed a more fundamental approach. He appealed in November, 1832, to the people of all the states to convene a constitutional convention charged to provide protection for *all* minority interests. That was far too visceral, and few people gave him their serious attention or thought. And so it ended with slavery more deeply entrenched (and even less ameliorated by personal relationships), a lower tariff, and a legacy of embittered determination among many southerners.

Those people paid little heed to Jackson's pious assertion in his Farewell Message that sectional differences must be adjusted, for otherwise the end of the Union would mean "an end to the hopes of freedom." They listened instead to Calhoun's warnings about "the extent and magnitude of the existing danger." "We are reposing on a volcano," he wrote, and if the pressure is not relieved it will "make *two people of one.*"

## VI

The interrelated crises deeply disturbed John Quincy Adams, and in 1839 he belatedly did what he should have done during the Missouri Crisis. He offered three amendments to the Constitution designed to end slavery over the next two generations. He suffered Calhoun's fate. But he was one of those rare conservatives who grow more radical with the years, and he shortly returned to discuss the central issue in a way that no one could ignore.

Rising in the House of Representatives on the morning of January 25, 1842, Adams read a petition from forty-six citizens of Haverhill, Massachusetts, who respectfully prayed for the Congress to adopt "measures peaceably to dissolve the Union of these States." He defended it by reference to the Declaration of Independence. "If there is a principle sacred on earth . . . it is the right of people to alter, to change, to destroy, the Government if it becomes oppressive to them."

The House became a shambles of consternation, anger, and outrage. There were a few references to showing respect for the views of an ex-President, but it was mostly a nasty debate. A motion to censure him was followed by one to send him home in disgrace to Massachusetts. It was a very lively time. Perhaps the most revealing remarks came from Joseph Rogers Underwood of Kentucky. Self-determination was all very well as a matter of theory, he admitted, but in practice it would destroy the American way of life.

"How could we retain our slaves, when they, in one hour, one day, or a week at the furthest, could pass the boundary." Nor was it a limited threat. "Sooner or later, this process would extend itself farther and farther south, rendering slave labor so precarious and uncertain that it could not be depended upon." "Slavery in the States would fall with the Union."

A few friends helped Adams mount his counteroffensive, but it was largely his own happy work. Some reported that he dropped twenty years in a fortnight. He relished his victory when the charges were withdrawn. Henry Clay remembered the lessons from that episode (and other encounters with Adams), and reiterated them a decade later as a somber warning to those who advocated intervention around the globe.

And a younger man, who was fond of citing Clay as his mentor and idol, probably learned as much from Calhoun and Adams as he did from the charismatic gentleman from Lexington. He was graced with an unusually powerful mind, driven by vaulting ambition, and quick to learn the shrewd expertise of politics; and he revealed exceptional skill with the language, a persistent taste for the mystical, and disturbingly sly habits. His name was Abraham Lincoln. He was little known beyond the secondary politics of Illinois during the eventful years between 1828 and 1838, but at the end of that period he gave two remarkable speeches that were as little clouds arising from the sea.[7]

Those who attended the Springfield YMCA Lyceum Lecture in 1838, for example, and listened carefully, got an earful. Lincoln began by revealing his keen awareness of the crisis in the East. He was concerned with "the perpetuation of our political institution," and it was time to realize that the Founding Fathers had not spoken the last word or solved

[7] The mind-opening commentary is by Edmund Wilson in *Eight Essays* (New York, Doubleday, 1954). Wilson's perceptions were belatedly explored by Harry V. Jaffa, *Crisis of the House Divided. An Interpretation of the Lincoln-Douglas Debates* (Seattle, U. of Washington Press, 1959), in a way more favorable to Lincoln. Inexplicably, the whole matter is ignored by Don E. Fehrenbacher, *Prelude to Greatness. Lincoln in the 1850s* (Stanford, Calif., Stanford U. Press, 1962).

all the problems. They were *"once* hardy, brave, and patriotic, but *now* a lamented and departed race of ancestors." Their "experiment is successful," but their work is done. Then Lincoln indulged his deadly skill with words. He seems laudatory, but is in truth neither respectful, kindly, nor considerate: their achievement is "not much to be wondered at." A classic disparagement as a throwaway line.

In any event, he continued, that "game is caught," and hence there remain no pleasures in that arena. Perpetuating their work is a routine exercise. A *real* man seeks his own and greater fields of the Lord. Next a blunt warning that such a man will seek vast powers to prove his mettle— and exercise his will. *He will, indeed, deny the right of free speech (hence self-determination) to those he considers wrong.* It was a majestic statement of the imperial ethic— my way is better than yours and I will therefore impose my way—masked in the rhetoric of law and order. And he had already said that slavery is "founded on both injustice and bad policy."

One cannot escape the kind of eerie recognition that comes upon one in the center of a storm at sea: Lincoln had set himself against Calhoun. Some man, he concluded, will satisfy his craving for distinction "whether at the expense of emancipating slaves, or enslaving free men." But while Calhoun might ask for equal treatment in the territories and ultimately defend slavery as a positive good, his primary objective was to honor the right of self-determination. Lincoln had already begun to distort the issue.

A few years later, in 1842, Lincoln underscored all those characteristics. He *was* a most nervy man. He dared to reveal the truth about his views and his intentions on the assumption that no one would understand the frightening —even appalling—things he was saying so slowly and so calmly. In truth, an arrogant man. Ostensibly talking about temperance, he again gave himself away to anyone who listened carefully. Use "a drop of honey," he advised, to catch the prize. Southerners remembered his advocacy of that strategy when he talked later about leaving slavery alone where it exists—confident that it would be destroyed by such containment.

His true object is to reform everyone—America first and then the world. To rid mankind of booze is good, but as nothing compared to giving the American Present to the rest of mankind. America discovered the answer to the question of self-government, and that truth will "grow and expand into the universal liberty of mankind." Oh, "Happy day, when, all appetites controlled, all passions subdued, all matters subjected. . . ."

And "when the victory shall be complete—when there shall be neither a slave nor a drunkard on the earth—how proud the title of that Land, which many truly claim to be the birthplace and the cradle of both those revolutions, that shall have ended in that victory." Later events reinforced the skepticism generated by those speeches about Lincoln's commitment to the right of self-determination.

# 5
# The Manifest Destiny
# of the American Present

Sir, we live in strange times. Revolutions of
Government, and the dismemberment of
empires . . . have of late become quite common
incidents.
    —Senator L. W. Tazewell of Virginia, 1831

I swear to do my utmost to promote Republican
Institutions and ideas throughout the world.
    —From the Oath of the Crusading Members of the
    New York Hunters Lodge, c. 1832

I am determined to vindicate the claims of the
present against those of the past.
    —Frontier Preacher, 1848

Those who are not for us are against us.
    —Senator Henry Stuart Foote of Mississippi, 1851

    Lincoln aside, many other people continued to reveal
their own reservations about revolutions that did not follow
the American pattern. The sense of isolation that underlay

that response was thereby reinforced in a way that contributed significantly to the rise of a spirit of aggressive expansionism. If other people could not create the Present out of the Past, then Americans would have to accept the responsibility and get on with the enterprise.

That approach seemed to succeed in Mexico (at least in the northern third of that country), but it quickly became apparent that it might well be the kind of success that in the end defines failure. Even so, other revolutions proved so disappointing that they posed the temptation of intervening to set them straight. All in all, the commitment to the principle of self-determination became increasingly inconvenient —if not dangerous—to the work of preserving the Present.

# I

Perhaps no one caught the persistent spirit of uneasiness better than Senator Littleton Waller Tazewell of Virginia. The revolutions in Europe and the continuing ferment in the Western Hemisphere disturbed him most seriously. "We live in strange times," he told the Senate in February, 1831. "Revolutions of Government, and the dismemberment of empires . . . have of late become quite common incidents. . . . It becomes us to look well to the ship in which our all is embarked." He was deeply worried that President Jackson would deal with the roil and rumble in a way that would lead to a foreign war. Tazewell was unusually perceptive. Jackson would have dealt with the developing crisis between Texas and Mexico in the way that later provoked a *domestic* conflict if he had not been deterred by his sense that he might start a civil war.

Jackson was also cautious in responding to the revolutionary stirrings in Canada, which served to encourage the annexationist talk that had been initiated by the editors of the *North American Review.* The fire-eaters in New York and elsewhere viewed Canada as a good place to begin acting on their oath "to do my utmost to promote Republican Institutions and Ideas throughout the world." Their emotions were all of a piece; and so, when the Canadians settled for more autonomy within the British Empire, they were denounced as "cowards and traitors."

The French were no better. Their revolution of 1830 was initially welcomed because of its concern with liberty of the press and its opposition to the machinations of the Pope and his cohorts in Rome. Even Jackson praised French "courage and wisdom." But it soon proved to be another disappointment. The French rested content with less than the American Present. And then that failure was compounded by their refusal to go to war to help the Polish revolutionaries.

The failure to aid the Poles was considered especially disgraceful because the Poles had timed their uprising to thwart what was thought to be a gathering Russian intervention against the French. The Poles were primarily concerned, of course, with securing their own independence, but their tactical decision evoked much respect and sympathy. So did the memories of Tadeusz Kosciuszko and Kazimierz Pulaski, who had fought with the colonists during the American Revolution.

The Polish patriots stood their ground against the Russians through ten months of bloody war. Americans quickly became excited, and a surprising number talked of military intervention. Edgar Allan Poe was only the most famous person who offered to volunteer, for example, and James Fenimore Cooper became a vigorous organizer in the campaign to provide material support. But the great majority preferred to stay at home and intervene by damning the Czar and spitting spiteful curses at the French for refusing to send their army eastward in behalf of freedom.[1]

Jackson was sympathetic, but far more concerned with exploiting the possibilities for expanding the American marketplace that were opened by the changes in France. His effort to enlarge trade with the French West Indies bespoke the growing propensity among Americans to link support for the principle of self-determination with the export of their surpluses. For the moment, however, they emphasized the ties between their desire for more land, the unique American mission to carry Christian civilization to backward peoples, and the necessity of preserving the Present.[2]

# II

All those elements came together in Texas. Americans first moved into that Mexican province during the economic downturn of 1819–22, and their success attracted an increasing number of settlers (and related commercial interests) during the following decade. The trouble erupted when the Mexican government attempted in 1830 to abolish slavery and to terminate further immigration from the United States. The Mexicans viewed Texas as part of their country that could be developed as a strong barricade against American expansion. The Americans in residence considered Texas to be an extension of the United States—or as the heartland of their own empire stretching west to the Pacific.

---

[1] This story is nicely outlined by J. J. Lerski, *A Polish Chapter in Jacksonian America* (Madison, Wisc., U. of Wisconsin Press, 1958).

[2] A perceptive and straightforward discussion of this explosive combination is offered by Frederick Merk, *Manifest Destiny and Mission in American History* (New York, Alfred A. Knopf, 1963). I do not, however, agree with his explanation of why it did not result in an attempt to conquer everything from Panama to the North Pole.

The serious shooting began in the summer of 1835, and within a year (on March 2, 1836) the Texans declared for independence. The loss of the Alamo at the end of a classic siege was avenged by Sam Houston in the battle of San Jacinto, and on October 22, 1836, he took the presidential oath of office. Most people in the United States viewed it all as a perfect example of how the principle of self-determination should work out in practice. Well, almost; at least until it came time to complete the process by adding Texas to the American Present.

That seemingly natural conclusion to the story contained a threat to the Present. For the antislavery people, along with the abolitionists, posed the specter of secession—or war—if Texas was acquired. Lincoln was not the only one who read it right. But Calhoun disdained to play Illinois games, and laid it out on the table: "It is easy to see the end. . . . We must become two people." Jackson badly wanted Texas but knew it involved grave risks. So he eased into it: he recognized Texas as a self-determined state in March, 1837, and left the rest to his successors.

The rest took ten years. Texas was finally annexed in 1845, and shortly thereafter President James K. Polk sent American troops into a disputed region as a means of self-determining a larger American empire. The Mexicans resisted that act of aggression in the name of their right to self-determine Mexico, and Polk had his war.[3] It ended in 1848

---

[3] Polk had decided to go to war before the Mexicans responded to the American blockade of their forces on the Rio Grande. Their move allowed him to pose as the innocent victim of unwarranted aggression. Lincoln, then an incidental congressman on the prowl for an issue to dramatize his presence, launched an attack on Polk for claiming the disputed territory as American. It did little to advance his career; but, given his later maneuver around Fort Sumter, one cannot avoid the thought that he learned from Polk how to act in a way that would start a war while shifting the blame to one's opponent. On the other hand, he may not have needed any instruction in such matters.

with America in possession of Mexico north of the Rio Grande and west to the harbor at San Diego. Americans had again preserved the Present. And in the process refined the mystique of the City on a Hill. It was an impressive performance, judge it as you will. For the themes of isolation, uniqueness, mission, expansion, and self-determination were reintegrated in a brilliant phrase—Manifest Destiny.

The man who coined that magical incantation was John L. O'Sullivan, an explosive advocate, as he phrased it, "for the development of the great experiment of liberty and self-government." At least as long as the self-government was defined the American way. He spoke for all the millions caught up in a religious revival to glorify and extend American civilization. As with Sam Houston, for example: Mexicans were an inferior people governed by "brigands and despots." Or the citizens of Illinois who knew that "extension and expansion is the condition of our political existence." And others in Louisiana who understood that American commercial expansion would "carry peace and comfort to every man's door." And those in Boston who declared that America carried "the hopes of humanity" on its shoulders. Senator Daniel S. Dickinson of New York provided an appropriate summation: "new races are presented for us to civilize, educate, and absorb."

John Quincy Adams was terribly disturbed by that booming "spirit of aggrandizement," and by the way in which Polk had established a precedent for maneuvering the country into war. But he and others like him were dismissed as part of the Bad Old Past. It was not so easy, however, to ignore the Frenchmen who went to the barricades in 1848 in an effort to hold off the Past while the Future was born. Tazewell had said it well: "We live in strange times." The world had become very complicated. The challenge of the Past was reinforced by the appearance of the Future.

Even more disturbing, the Present itself was threatened by a visceral struggle to control the trans-Mississippi west.

## III

Representative David Wilmot of Pennsylvania proposed on August 6, 1846, to prohibit slavery in any part of the empire acquired from Mexico. Calhoun replied early in 1847: the basic right of self-determination insured the people of each state the right to establish their own government and institutions, even those that other people considered misguided or mistaken. If that principle was violated, the southern states would separate and go their own way. "All we ask is to be let alone; but if trampled upon, it will be idle to expect that we will not resist it."

That was a frightful threat to the Present, and Americans quickly ducked off to immerse themselves in a new wave of European revolutions. The Germans generated some initial enthusiasm in 1848 (as in New York and Richmond, and in Boston and New Orleans), but it quickly dissipated in the general disgust with their ineffectualness. All they did was talk. It was disappointing, but it confirmed the feeling among a growing number of Americans that no one else could make a proper revolution. It was all something of a joke: "moonstruck professors" who were "drunk on liberty" could not be expected to bring the Past into the Present.

Then the French again offered hope that America was not alone. They started well enough, and popular rallies helped to push the Congress to begin considering in March, 1848, a resolution of sympathy and congratulations. But then some French people displayed a determination to move on into the Future. They not only talked about socialism and communism, they established what Americans considered a commune.

That was intolerable. The triumph of "Mob Government," screamed the Washington *National Intelligencer*, over a proper system of "Law and Order." Southerners were appalled by the prospect of "Socialism!" But northerners were equally disturbed by a movement that anticipated "the upturning and overthrow" of capitalism. Part of that reaction can be explained by the popular attraction of romanticism. For the belief that only the individual could change the world was in truth a most conservative outlook: a gilding of the dandelion of individualistic capitalism.[4] And so it reinforced the fear of the Future.

Southerners like Representative Henry Washington Hilliard of Alabama wasted few words: the French were too willing "to plunge into the wild, unrestricted, and reckless experiment of ideal Liberty." Many others shared the fear that "regulated liberty" would be dishonored. Senator William Lewis Dayton of New Jersey, for example, fretted about those who were willing to pander "to the passions of the populace." The French were simply unable to recognize and act on the principles of true civilization. And more than a few agreed with Senator Samuel S. Phelps who asserted that it was time to stop worrying about the right of self-determination because otherwise America would fall victim to "fanatical theories in our own country."

That gentleman may have been worrying as much about the Women's Rights Convention that opened in Senecca, New York, on July 19, 1848, as about the French radicals. In any event, it was all of a piece: preserve the American Present. And, fresh from his conquests in Mexico, President Polk exuded confidence: "Our blessed country," he announced in December, "presents a sublime moral spectacle to the world."

---

[4] One of the most perceptive essays is J. L. Thomas, "Romantic Reform in America: 1815–1865," *American Quarterly*, Vol. 17 (1965), pp. 656–681.

## IV

There did remain, however, a few ideological and practical difficulties. They were dramatized, and woven together, around events in central Europe. Turning away from the French in horror and disgust, Americans focused their hopes and enthusiasms upon the revolutionaries in Hungary who sought independence from Austria. Some Americans on the scene in Vienna when violence first erupted in March, 1848, feared that the people were not ready for freedom, but the vast majority of their countrymen hailed the uprising as another American Revolution.[5]

The Hungarians offered unlimited possibilities: expanded trade; a chance to punish Russia (as well as Austria) for all its sins; and an opportunity to indulge one's penchant for apocalyptic visions. The fate of Europe for centuries to come hung in the balance; and even if the Hungarians caused a general war, it would be worth that price to put an end to the Past.

Horace Greeley of the New York *Tribune* argued for intervention as "the agent of Providence" to republicanize Europe. The *Democratic Review* stressed the chance to expand the market for American surpluses. Senator John Jordan Crittenden of Kentucky called for a strong policy to assert the American Present against "the pride and presumption of the Old World." That "would please our people," he added, an observation based on the widespread public furor. Perhaps the biggest demonstration took place in New York City

[5] Here consult Merle E. Curti, *Austria and the United States, 1848–1852. Smith College Studies in History*, Vol. 11 (1926); and Arthur J. May, *Contemporary American Opinion of the Mid-Century Revolutions in Central Europe* (Philadelphia, n.p., 1927). Both volumes are extremely helpful and complement each other. But the Curti study is a remarkable example of brilliance prefigured: he wrote it as an undergraduate.

under a banner proclaiming "Freedom of the world," but there was intense agitation throughout the country.

President Zachary Taylor, whose bold advance into Mexico helped him to reach the White House, responded with a probe into the heart of Europe. The administration ordered an official then in France to scout the situation and, if warranted, recognize the revolutionaries and negotiate favorable commercial treaties. The agent arrived after the Austrians had defeated the Hungarians, but the intent and the attempt produced a confrontation that sustained the issue long after the last rifle had been fired for the last time.

The ensuing turmoil is one of the most illuminating episodes in American history. For it not only dramatized the intense sense of unique mission and the deep fear of isolation, but it revealed to some Americans that intervention in the name of self-determination posed some potentially unhappy consequences. And that awareness led on to a decision to modify the principle so that it would not subvert the American Present.

It is necessary to keep in mind, as we wiggle our way through those tangled vines, that the Hungarians had been defeated and that their most charismatic leader, Louis Kossuth, had been incarcerated at Austria's insistence in a Turkish prison. Those facts define the stage of the drama and also reveal the psychological state of America. One has the eerie feeling of being in the company of people who have become so involved in a play *that is over* that they immediately proceed to write and perform another act.

Certainly the vast majority of Americans had identified that deeply with the Hungarian revolutionaries. Their anger at Austria pushed the Congress into a revealing debate about rescuing Kossuth, and suspending diplomatic relations with Vienna, as acts to further the expansion of freedom. The Taylor Administration's campaign to free Kossuth prob-

101

WILLIAM APPLEMAN WILLIAMS

ably contributed to his eventual release, but the pressure from England was more effective. (But not, of course, in the view of contemporary Americans.) The strategy of a diplomatic rupture, however, was wholly American.

It is no doubt true that Senator Lewis Cass of Michigan was moved by his desire to occupy the White House when, in January, 1850, he introduced his resolution to condemn Austria to diplomatic limbo. But the important point is that he considered the action appropriate to the objective. He wanted "to rebuke . . . atrocious acts of despotism" and he mustered significant support.

One of those who supported Cass even provided a preview of a proposal advanced almost a century later by Woodrow Wilson. "It is the province, the mission, aye, the destiny" of America to "become a propagandist . . . an emissary" of The American Truth. The United States should also break relations with Russia and extend the Monroe Doctrine to the world. That was the only way to finish off the Bad Old Past. Senator William Henry Seward of New York added his praise for a speech "so eloquent, upon principles so noble, and discussing a policy so great."

Others agreed, but thought that was precisely the trouble. Senator John Parker Hale of New Hampshire was willing to consider a crusade at home, but unwilling to take on the world. He was the first openly antislavery candidate to be elected to the Senate, and he knew how to make a point. All right, he began, we are proposing "to erect ourselves into a high court. . . . We are to arraign at our bar the nations of the world . . . and we are to pass judgment upon them." Well and good, let us begin by severing relations with Russia as punishment for suppressing the Poles and then work our way down the endless list of transgressors.

His colleague Robert M. T. Hunter of Virginia provided effective support. If that was the meaning of self-

102

determination, then we had been inexcusably remiss: "Why sir, we could not have recalled ministers fast enough." He agreed with Cass and Seward that America was the greatest nation in the world but denied that even that unique virtue gave it "the right to supervise and control" the internal affairs of other countries. There was nothing "more arrogant and insulting. It is a virtual denial of the sovereignty of the foreign State."

Hunter was unquestionably thinking about the increasingly difficult position of Virginia and other slave states at home. Led by Calhoun, a significant number of their influential spokesmen had issued on January 22, 1849, another warning that they were prepared to act upon their right of self-determination. The new Secretary of State, Daniel Webster, did not have to be reminded. He knew that the southerners were serious and that Calhoun had long ago posed the central question.[6]

And so he tried to use the appeal of the American mission to save the world to subvert the commitment to the right of self-determination. The Austrians had understandably protested the move to recognize the Hungarian revolutionaries and were additionally annoyed by the wildly enthusiastic reception accorded to Kossuth when he arrived in America.[7] Encouraged by William Hunter, a clerk in the State Department, Webster issued a flaming manifesto of America's destiny to preserve the Present.

The United States was wholly justified in expressing its "warm sympathy" for those who were struggling to break free of the chains of the Past; and Austria should realize that, compared to America, it was "but a patch on the earth's sur-

[6] Robert F. Dalzell, Jr., *Daniel Webster and the Trial of American Nationalism, 1843–1852* (Boston, Houghton Mifflin, 1973) offers a keen insight into this aspect of Webster.
[7] I have not discussed that part of the story because it was merely an extension of the popular excitement previously noted.

face." Seward provided amplification. "The American Revolution terminated the dispute" about "the true theory of government." The discussion was closed. He worried about those who became so "carried away" that they thought there was a Future, but the first task was to finish off the Past.

It all sounded more than a bit like the rhetoric that Henry Clay had popularized in his heyday. But Clay had learned from John Quincy Adams, and from his own reflection, and knew that it was not that simple. "Sir," he warned, "any interference" with peoples struggling to exercise their right of self-determination is highly dangerous. "We have only to reverse the positions . . . to appreciate it. Suppose any one of the States in this Union was in a state of revolt against the Central Government, and any European Power should send an agent here for the purpose of obtaining information . . . certainly it would create a great deal of feeling throughout the United States."

Clay was answered by Senator Henry Stuart Foote of Mississippi. Foote was a southerner who opposed secession, and so his argument proved doubly ironic. He prophesied in nine simple words the demise of the commitment to the right of self-determination at home *and* abroad.

"Those who are not for us are against us."

# 6

# Honest Abe
# and the First Crusade
# to Save the Present

This Union must be a voluntary one, and
not compulsory. A union upheld by force would
be despotism.

—William Henry Seward, 1840

All that we ask of you is, keep your hands
out of our pockets.

—Representative Alexander H. Stephens<br>of Georgia, 1854

I believe this government cannot endure permanently,
half slave and half free. I do not expect the Union
to be dissolved. I do not expect the house to fall;
but I do expect it will cease to be divided.
It will become all one thing or all the other.

—Abraham Lincoln, 1858

Never forget that we have before us this
whole matter of the right or wrong of slavery.

—Abraham Lincoln, 1859

Lincoln was always precise to almost a unique degree
in his statements, and it is interesting to note
that he did not say that it was not his object
to destroy slavery.
> —Historian David M. Potter, 1968

If the Declaration of Independence be true
(and who here gainsays it?) every community
may dissolve its connection with any other
community previously made.
> —Jefferson Davis, 1861

The contest is really for empire on the side of
the North, and for independence on that
of the South.
> —London *Times*, 1861

In any case, I think our slave property will be
lost eventually.
> —Jefferson Davis to his wife, 1861

The currents of fear and foreboding that developed within the enthusiasm about the European revolutions of the 1830s and 1840s bespoke an awareness that the Present was being challenged by the Future as well as the Past. That was as true within America as in Europe. The abolitionists not only threatened southerners, but posed an almost equally unhappy prospect for the vast majority of northerners who had no interest in competing with—or living next to —a free Black person. Others viewed the radical efforts to construct Socialist or related communities as also threatening the essence of the Present.

Nor was that all. The defeat of Mexico and the conquest of the Southwest rounded out the continental empire, but that success raised a central problem. For if democratic republicanism depended upon expansion, then the Present could only be preserved by more wars to "expand the area of freedom." That was troublesome enough, but it also underscored the danger posed by the South. There had always been two Presents within America, and now both of them had developed to the point of being able to sustain their independence.

As Melville realized, Americans were after all no more than ordinary mortals—not unique, not graced with a special mission, and not a better hope than anyone else.[1] This was a frightening moment of recognition shared by ever more leaders in the North; for southerners appeared increasingly ready to strike out on their own. It was all very well, and reassuring, to damn them for slavery, and accuse them of running a bluff, but they continued to display unmistakable signs of being committed to exercising their inalienable right to go to hell in their own way—even unto the demise of slavery in the name of independence.

Terrifying. So unnerving that many northerners tried to tranquilize themselves by treating the prospect as the chimera of disordered (or evil) minds. It would mean, as Clay cried out in anguish on February 6, 1850, "the extinction of this last and glorious light which is leading all mankind." Two northern intellectual leaders, Francis Lieber and Joseph Parrish Thompson, took the argument another step. The right of revolutionary self-determination, they asserted, was "qualified and conditional." They were but staff officers in an army command by Lincoln. Read him carefully—*very carefully*—and he deserves the nickname of Honest Abe. But take him at one glance, or listen to him with but one ear, and you think he is saying something rather different from

---

[1] Here see the analysis by Loren Baritz, *City on a Hill* (New York, John Wiley & Sons, 1964), p. 331, and the entire chapter.

his real message. And one has to read him that closely, because he wrote that precisely.

Lincoln ultimately achieved his ambition to displace Washington as the Father of the Country. He became the Bloodied Savior of the American Present. He concluded that the northern way of life could not survive unless it honored Madison's conception of the right of self-determination as an imperial ethic: to remain the world's best hope, that is, America must assert America's version of self-determination as mankind's definition of self-determination. After the revolutions of the 1840s, moreover, he asserted that America was not just the "best hope," but was the "last best hope." Jefferson's assertion of missionary uniqueness had become apocalyptic.

# I

Lincoln's willfulness was focused by Calhoun's challenge.[2] He saw it for what it was: a double threat. For to honor the principle of revolutionary self-determination by allowing the South to develop in its own way into its own Future meant to risk losing all: uniqueness, mission, and prosperity—even one's place in history. And it was a real, not merely a theoretical, threat. Calhoun thought in abstract terms, but his ideas and proposals struck deep into the guts of the issue; and the South emerged from the turmoil of the 1840s ever more clearly displaying a prerevolutionary psychology. It shortly became revolutionary.

The long and bitter fight to organize the House of

[2] I leave the formalistic analysis of the physiological and psychoanalytical origins of Lincoln's inordinate ambition to the experts. For openers, consult Norman Kiell (ed.), *Psychological Studies of Famous Americans, The Civil War Era* (New York, Twayne, 1964). I also recommend one of my favorites: Richard Current, *The Lincoln Nobody Knows* (New York, Hill & Wang, 1958).

Representatives in December, 1849, revealed many expressions of that dynamic process. Jeremiah Clemens of Alabama put it as well as any: "We do not intend to stand still and have our throats cut. The Union is valuable only for the privileges it confers and the rights it secures." That blunt warning, along with many others that had been offered since 1828, provided the foundation for John F. Kennedy's later observation that the Confederate Revolution was "not the suddenly inspired project of the present day." Another southerner explained it all in terms that would earn high marks from the masters of sociology: "The causes lay far deeper and were to be found in antagonisms of character and interest; in distinctive differences of habit, character modes of thought, political dissent, and ideas of government radically and irreconcilably opposed."

The self-consciousness of the South was based on its long development as a viable subculture. The people of that area shared, and prided themselves upon, the fundamental commonalities of food, the life of the soil, related ethnic backgrounds, and a regional humor—and mores. There was, furthermore, a directness—even primalness—in the relationship between the people and the land; and also what has been called a special "personalism in the relations of man to man" that affected even the relationship between master and slave. Within that culture, moreover, radicalism and egalitarianism existed alongside hierarchical conservatism.[3]

The political economy of the South underpinned and did much to shape and intensify that sense of separateness and increasing isolation and weakness within the federal sys-

[3] On these matters, see Jesse T. Carpenter, *The South as a Conscious Minority* (Gloucester, Mass., Peter Smith, 1930); Avery O. Craven, *The Growth of Southern Nationalism, 1848–1861* (Baton Rouge, La., Louisiana State U. Press, 1968); and William R. Taylor, *Cavalier and Yankee. The Old South and American National Character* (New York, George Braziller, 1961); along with the debates in the Congress and the private records of southerners.

tem. The visceral feelings were captured by Representative Alexander H. Stephens in one earthy sentence: "All that we ask of you is, keep your hands out of our pockets." Jefferson Davis made the point in the classic language of political theory: "The planting states have a common interest of such magnitude that their union, sooner or later, for the protection of that interest, is certain."

The powerful psychological forces toward independence that were generated by those realities were reinforced by events in Europe. It was not simply—or even primarily— that the Paris radicals cast a futuristic red shadow across the Present; it was that the era of the soil and of men governing themselves through face-to-face dealings in relatively small groups seemed doomed. Everywhere good people were either giving over with a shrug or displaying an appalling incompetence to sustain that kind of life.[4]

Then Harriet Beecher Stowe published *Uncle Tom's Cabin.* It aroused the North and fused the South. The chain reaction had begun. Guerrilla war erupted in Kansas: the first violence which dramatized the long simmering struggle to determine which Present would control the Western empire. And the South lost. Then John Brown. Having murdered privately in Kansas, he found funding among the philanthropists of the North, and killed again in Virginia, hoping to ignite a Black uprising.

One troubled yeoman in North Carolina provided the clue to all that was to come: those events have "shaken my fidelity and . . . I am willing to take the chances of every probable evil that may arise from disunion, sooner than submit any longer to Northern insolence and Northern outrage." No wonder at all that William L. Yancey of South Carolina thought the time was ripe for organizing (shades of 1772)

[4] Here again see Taylor, *Cavalier and Yankee,* especially pp. 52, 55, 62–63, and 96–101.

Committees of Safety to "precipitate the cotton States into a revolution."

## II

And then came Abraham Lincoln. Honest Abe from Illinois: full of ruthless righteousness about the "monstrous injustice of slavery," full of fears about the inability of the North to survive on its own, full of missionary zeal to globalize the American solution to life, and full of ambition to transcend the Founding Fathers.

Many southerners read him right. That says a good bit about their intellectual powers and their political savvy, for Lincoln was a Houdini with words. He used them magisterially to mask the truth that he was abroad upon a grand voyage to honor his slyly limited commitment to the revolutionary right of self-determination. He was more than a bit arrogant, telling all those who criticized or fretted to reread his speeches in the confidence they would miss the central point.

But recall one of his major statements of ostensible fidelity to that first principle. "Any people anywhere," he began on January 12, 1848, "being inclined and having the power, have the *right* to rise up, and shake off the existing government, and form a new one that suits them better. This is a most valuable,—a most sacred right—a right, which we hope and believe, is to liberate the world. Nor is this right confined to cases in which the whole people of an existing government, may choose to exercise it. Any portion of such people that *can, may* revolutionize, and make their *own*, of so much of the territory as they inhabit." [5]

[5] It is revealing to note a significant difference between this statement and his seemingly similar one of three days earlier: on January 9 he did not use the crucial modifying phrase "having the power."

Reading that passage with the mandatory caution, one sees two revealing passages. The first refers to the concern that the exercise of the right of revolutionary self-determination will "liberate the world." As far as Lincoln was concerned, America had forever settled the question of the best form of government. It was therefore the "last best hope of earth." Hence the right of revolution could liberate the world only if it was used to emulate *his* America.

The second caveat is the subtle reservation about the right of all or a part of the people to determine their own way of life. They *may* if they *can*. That is obvious, so the question arises: why raise the point when ostensibly discussing the *right* of revolution? Lincoln is advancing the right of counterrevolution in the name of *his* American good, just as in 1838 he advocated the right of suppressing free speech when it was being used in behalf of a cause *he* considered wrong.

So we must ask very seriously whether or not Lincoln was unequivocally committed to the principle of revolutionary self-determination. Was he willing to let it happen as it would? The answer is no. He was committed only to the preservation of *his* Present. He was intent upon—and had been since at least 1838—destroying slavery and the South.

That did not mean that Lincoln accepted Black people as equals. He did not. He preferred to be rid of them, and only very reluctantly accepted the necessity of coexistence. He was the personification of the antislavery mentality as opposed to the spirit of egalitarian abolitionism. That was the key to his success, for there were many northerners who were antislavery because the southern political economy posed a threat to *their* way of life—and only a thimbleful of egalitarian abolitionists. Honest Abe can realistically be called the prophet of segregation. Leave them alone, he advised. Which means in practice abandoning them to the terrors of a marketplace dominated by whites.

Or consider the House Divided speech. Lincoln will not allow the Union to be dissolved. The South will be contained, and that will lead to its death. It was not an eccentric view. Not even original. Congressman Columbus Delano of Ohio, for example, stated the theory very clearly: "We will establish a cordon of free States that shall surround you; and then we will light up the fires of liberty on every side, until they melt your present chains, and render all your people free. This is no idle boast." It was the ultimate appeal to the genius of Madison: expand or die. Hence if we keep you from expanding you will die.

# III

Put simply, the cause of the Civil War was the refusal of Lincoln and other northerners to honor the revolutionary right of self-determination—the touchstone of the American Revolution.[6] It is important to assert and reassert the evil of slavery, a truth with which I agree, but that will not enable one to wriggle off the hook. The act of imposing one people's morality upon another people is an imperial denial of self-determination. Once begin the process of denying it to others in its own name and there is no end of empire except war and more war.

Push it through the eye of the needle. It is the right and responsibility of Blacks—and any other people, including ourselves—to self-determine themselves. We save ourselves in the hope that we can then come together to create a community.

Give Honest Abe his due. He did toy with a hard answer. He was so intelligent that he could not forever evade it, and he first sidled up to it in 1854 during a speech

[6] For a learned and sophisticated review of the orthodox debate about this issue, see Eric Foner, "The Causes of the Civil War: Recent Interpretations and New Direction," *Civil War History,* Vol. 20 (1974), pp. 197–214.

in Peoria. Slavery was evil, he began, and it threatened the perpetuation of the northern way of life. Even so, it might be wise to devise a way to end it without a monstrous war. Accept a "GREAT evil" in the short run "to avoid a GREATER one." Then in 1858 he looked that "very important question" more nearly in the eye. If we could agree to stop all expansion, then we might work it out without violence. Finally, as he was about to take the power he had stalked for a lifetime, he confronted Madison without flinching. There was one compromise, he commented on January 11, 1861, that would be satisfactory. "A prohibition against acquiring any more territory."

But Lincoln never pushed that solution while he was hacking out his trail to the White House, and he did not use his power and prestige as President-elect to move it forward and secure its adoption. He might have lost. But we must judge such men by what they try—or do not try. Instead, Lincoln said only to play it tough. Let there be no compromise: "Have none of it." That would reduce America, he warned, to "the existing disorganized state of affairs in Mexico." And so came the end of the revolutionary right of self-determination. "My opinion is that no state can, in any way lawfully, get out of the Union, without the consent of the others."

A pathetic quibble. Hair splitting instead of rail splitting. Grant him a hope—even a fervent prayer or a mystical revelation—that the South would crumble. Acknowledge even, the pressures upon him to preserve the northern Present. Consider William Henry Seward, a persistent and by no means wholly defeated rival for supreme power. He had earlier said (in 1844 and again in 1848) that "a Union upheld by force would be a despotism." The true mission of America, he added, was "to demonstrate the reality of peaceful dissolution and friendly reconciliation." He soon took a different line. The North became all there was: "the ark of safety in which are deposited the hopes of the world." [7]

Senator Benjamin Wade of Ohio damned the South for its "backwardness." Others stressed Seward's point: the mission of the North was one of "developing, elevating, and reforming mankind." Ralph Waldo Emerson welcomed the prospect of war to enthrone laissez-faire individualism. Those less bold offered more mundane rationalizations. [8] And the unimaginative pragmatists assumed the worst without so much as a thought of negotiation. To lose New Orleans was to lose life. (Lincoln later used that argument as if he had invented it.)

The truth of it was that most northern leaders were frightened nearly out of their wits by the prospect of independence. [9] And so for courage they substituted mission. Save the North and save the world by saving the South. Perhaps nothing reveals the essential weakness of the North's position as clearly as the documents prepared by Seward under Lincoln's direction. For it was necessary, when distinguished European liberals were viewing the conflict as one involving self-determination and empire, to make the strongest possible case for empire. As one of those observers commented, it was "a struggle, on the one hand, for independence and self-government, on the other, for empire, political power, and material interests."

There were material interests, and expansionist urges, on *both* sides, but that does not meet the question about the South's right of self-determination. Seward's response, which we can reasonably assume did not become actionable until

[7] Lincoln must accept some responsibility for pushing Seward into this position, though Seward's crusading zeal might ultimately have carried him there of its own power.

[8] Here see George M. Frederickson, *The Inner Civil War. Northern Intellectuals and the Crisis of the Union* (New York, Harper & Row, 1965).

[9] Here see Phillip S. Paludan, "The American Civil War Considered as a Crisis in Law and Order," *American Historical Review*, Vol. 77 (1972), pp. 1013–1035.

Lincoln approved the fundamental lines of argument, took the form of basic instructions to key northern representatives in foreign countries.[10]

The first point of importance is that Seward, even though he occasionally used other terms, *consistently referred to secession and the creation of the Confederacy as a "revolution."* It was not so much a Freudian or a Marxian slip as it was an American slip.

Despite that giveaway, Seward never dealt seriously with the action as a revolution. All he says about southern activities as acts of self-determination is that they are "unpracticable," "unreasonable," "absurd," "unnecessary," and doomed to failure because of the superior power of the North.

He *explained* the revolution as being caused by the struggle between the North and the South for the trans-Mississippi empire. The South should have been content with what it had and allowed the North to take the rest. That was eminently reasonable, Seward continued, for the following reasons, which can only be understood by realizing that whenever he refers to the United States or America he is talking only about the North.

First, the establishment of the United States through the Revolutions of 1776 and 1787 solved forever the question of the best form of government and was therefore "the most auspicious political event that has happened in the whole progress of history."

Second, the success of the Confederate Revolution

---

[10] All the dispatches are extremely revealing, but I have developed the following reconstruction around three documents: Seward to Dayton (France), April 22, 1861; to Wood (The Netherlands), May 1, 1861; and to Clay (Russia), May 6, 1861. The precise extent of Lincoln's involvement is, in my opinion, impossible to determine; but the basic thrust of the argument is so similar to his earlier and current statements, and his concern to keep Seward on a very short leash is so well known, that I see no grounds for concluding that Seward was off turning outside loops on his own.

would lead to the "destruction of the safety, happiness, and welfare of the whole American people." That was because it would mean that America's "moral force was spent." Or, in other terms, "the loss of ambition . . . the loss of enterprise and vigor . . . the loss of sustained and constant culture . . . [and] the greatest calamity of all, the loss of liberty."

Sensing, perhaps, that the last reason posed a puzzler of major proportions (how to lose liberty by losing slavery), Seward offered his third answer. The failure to destroy the Confederacy would open the door to "anarchy, such as so widely prevails in Spanish America." That would lead to "the loss of the respect of mankind, and the veneration and respect of posterity."

Finally, and not at all least, the United States was charged with the mission of preserving peace and progress throughout the world. A Confederate success would so upset "the equilibrium of the nations, maintained by this republic," that no one could be sure that mankind would even have another chance. "The progress arrested, and the hopes of humanity . . . would be disappointed and indefinitely postponed."

Hence war. Of course it would be short and lead to reasonable surrender and reconciliation in the best interests of the United States as defined by the North.

## IV

Weak arguments and weaker perceptions of reality. The Confederacy was willing to take its chances—including the possibility that it would prove necessary to end slavery to secure independence and self-determination. Clay and others had candidly admitted, at least as early as 1850, that secession would open the door to freedom for "hundreds and thousands" of slaves. Be that as it may, Jefferson Davis said it once and for all to his wife in 1861: "In any case, I think our slave property will be lost eventually."

Slavery was a central feature of the southern subculture that asserted its right of revolutionary self-determination. And, once again, slavery is evil. But there is also a vital truth contained in the classical warning about the fallacy of misplaced concreteness. If all we think about is slavery, that is to say, then we overlook other issues that may be equally important. If southerners can walk through the door into independence knowing that it may mean the end of slavery,[11] then the rest of us should honor our commitment to the right of self-determination by letting them go in peace.

Some urged that course, and many others offered proposals for compromise. John Minor Botts of Virginia, for example, suggested a national convention to consider a constitutional amendment authorizing secession. Federal property would be pegged at a fair price and paid for over time. Some New Englanders, as in Connecticut, argued vigorously for honoring the right of peaceful separation. George W. Bassett of Illinois agreed: secession involved "the great natural and sacred right of self-government." And others acknowledged that "the secessionists are right in their main principle."

That jammed Lincoln and other crusaders into a corner. Wendell Phillips and Horace Greeley whined about the failure of the southerners to observe Constitutional procedures and ducked off into wretched equivocations and fantasies. They were dishonest. In comparison, one has to respect Seward. He was, at least in his better moments, majestically imperial. "The Union has not yet accomplished

---

[11] Beyond the candid remarks on the floor of the Congress, and in private correspondence, the point is nicely stated and developed by Robert F. Durden, *The Gray and the Black. The Confederate Debate on Emancipation* (Baton Rouge, La., Louisiana State U. Press, 1972).

what good for mankind was manifestly designed by Him who appoints the reasons and prescribes the duties of states and empires."

Lincoln was feeble. All he could say was that it was "too late." His worst moment. He had said repeatedly that he was willing to leave slavery alone where it was, but he proved unwilling to honor his own proposition. For leaving slavery alone where it was meant accepting secession. No way out of that box. No reason for him not to have done that, negotiated in good faith for fair compensation for federal property and egress through New Orleans, and proceeded with the development of the North. Leave the Confederacy to its fate. Fort Sumter is irrelevant if you have faith in the North.

The soul-wrenching truth of it is that Lincoln played a double game. He wanted to transcend the Founding Fathers, free the slaves, and expand America's power throughout the world. But he lacked the courage to take his chances on that program. He tried to confront himself in his Inaugural Address, and it is a fascinating document. He is there the ultimate personification of the Great Seal of the United States: warm, soft olive branches and cold, honed arrows. The ruthless crusader for peace.

But not even Lincoln could square the circle. It all came to nought because of the damnable revolutionary right of self-determination. He began with noble words about that principle, shied away, then returned, and finally gave it up for lost.[12] He knew the charade was over. He understood, even better than the editors of the London *Times*, that he had opted for empire. Hence, to return to his prophetic imagery of 1838, the new game had begun: the imperial game, in which the right of revolution would be invoked to justify counterrevolution.

[12] This vital point is nicely sensed by Frederickson, *The Inner Civil War*, p. 59.

# 7

# Visions of an American Global Commonwealth and the Realities of Empire

It is very well; you are building excellent states
to be hereafter admitted into the American Union.
—Senator William H. Seward of New York,
referring to Canadians, 1860

If nobody can lick us we need not be afraid
to play the just and generous big brother
among the nations.
—Reformer Henry Demarest Lloyd, c. 1885

I am an exporter, I want the world.
—Charles L. Lovering, textile manufacturer, 1890

If Cuba were free she would pass under
American trade influences.
—*People's Party Paper,* 1896

Lincoln might have become a myth even if he had
not been assassinated on the morrow of the crushing defeat
of the Confederacy. The terrors of the war—his war—left him
personally more humble and less insistent as a public figure

upon imposing his will upon other people. He found it impossible to be unaffected by the death of 617,528 people, and another 375,175 casualties. Given those changes, his exceptional intelligence and remarkable political skill might have solved the awesome problems of integrating southerners—Black and white—into the body politic. That achievement would have been the substance of a truly mythic place in history.

We will never know. John Wilkes Booth denied us that knowledge and left us with the need to believe it was true. Lincoln became our first unknown soldier, and hence we created the myth and built the tomb.

But, all that said, we have to face the truth that he steered a counterrevolutionary course. Hence the myth is dangerous because it obscures the truth. In such cases we are better left saying, "I wonder," rather than asserting that we know.

Lincoln's American Present was the possessive individualism of marketplace capitalism, and he riveted it upon America. That not only perpetuated the sense that expansionism was vital to America's well-being, but also reinforced the sense of unique mission to reform the world. And in the process he consolidated and extended all the earlier precedents for the President to use any and all powers at his discretion.

His vision of a global commonwealth modeled upon, and led by, the United States was sustained and elaborated by many people after he was murdered. It was not his creation, of course, but the nature of the war and his death unquestionably intensified the old belief in a special American mission. The remnants of the Bad Past had been expunged, and that proved America's uniqueness. And the terrible cost of that effort intensified the fervor to carry the truth to all peoples.

That conception of duty, along with the belief in the necessity of expansion, ultimately crushed whatever part of the original commitment to the revolutionary right of self-determination survived the war. The final subversion was sanctified in the name of the original principle, however, for only in that way could Americans come to terms with the reality of having become counterrevolutionaries.

## I

Once Lincoln was dead, Secretary of State Seward emerged as the great prophet of the global American commonwealth. He had been one of many such visionaries before the war, and even then the reach of his imagination and his verve marked him as exceptional. Just as he supported the suppression of Confederate independence in the name of "a Higher Law," so also he invoked "a Law of Providence" to explain the mission of the United States to expand and reform the world.

America was destined, Seward cried in 1852, to take charge of "the restoration of the unity of the human family." That would produce "our own complete emancipation from what remains of European influence and prejudice"—free us from the Past—"and in turn develop the American opinion and influence which shall remould constitutions, laws, and customs in [Asia] the land that is first greeted by the rising sun"—forever project the Present into the Future.

America was once again "the world's best hope." He praised the Canadians for "building excellent states to be hereafter admitted into the American Union"; and offered benevolent encouragement to the Mexicans, whose "rapid decay and dissolution" was but "the preparatory stage for their reorganization in free, equal, and self-governing mem-

122

bers of the United States of America." For that matter, Mexico City might even qualify as the capital of the American Global Commonwealth.

As for Russia, it was candidly warned of a future confrontation "in [Manchuria] the region where civilization first began, and where, after so many ages, it has become now lethargic and helpless." There was no doubt in Seward's mind that America would prove triumphant and thereby prevent the Past from ever again threatening the Present.

Although no other American quite matched Seward's ability to spin visions out of the silk of uniqueness, the cashmere of mission, and the flax of economic necessity, many others offered their own revelations. Even so proper and cautious a man as William M. Evarts, who also served as Secretary of State from 1877 to 1881, occasionally allowed himself to talk about the need for the United States to take the lead in keeping the peace of the world while other societies struggled along to reach its higher stage of development. But other prophets, confident in the defeat of the Confederacy and the freeing of the slaves, were far bolder (and more verbose) than Evarts.

Most of them, like Seward, stressed the religious elements of uniqueness and mission. John Fiske's essay of 1885 on Manifest Destiny, for example, invoked his version of Christianity as a sanction for carrying America's political theory and economic institutions to all the benighted of the globe. So also with Josiah Strong, whose *Our Country* (also 1885) became a best seller. His fear of the barbarous Past, and of an anarchic Future, led him to preach zealous sermons about the American mission. "The world is to be Christianized and civilized," and the United States is God's chosen instrument. Even Captain Alfred Thayer Mahan of the navy, whose later arguments for expansion emphasized economic necessities (and a strategy derived therefrom), spoke with deep conviction about America's Christian mission to save the world from a heathen Past.

Perhaps the most illuminating vision was offered, however, by the secular groups whose members were intensely concerned about their decreasing ability to self-determine their own lives in the American Present. The First Americans had from the beginning advocated sharing the vast spaces and resources of the continent, and they persistently clung to that dream after the defeat of the Confederacy. Leaders among the freed slaves, and other Black spokesmen in the North, likewise spoke of an America which would honor the ideal of equality. And the more radical members of the rapidly growing force of industrial workers advanced their own versions of a more humane America.

Those expressions of faith and hope about a golden Future were noble and significant, and they sustained many people through extremely difficult times in the Present. They believed that honoring the right of self-determination would enable Americans to transcend the possessive individualism of the capitalist marketplace and create an American community. But they were outnumbered—and outmuscled—by others who were reforging the traditional chain that bound the ideal of self-determination to the practice of empire.

Most of those people believed in the principle of self-determination. They did not begin as imperialists. Their evolution into advocates of empire is not a story of the triumph of Evil, but rather a tale of tragedy caused by the fear of the Future. The men and women in question were the farmers, who constituted the majority of Americans between 1865 and 1900, and their allies among the reformers of the cities. They saw their own right of self-determination being progressively circumscribed by a minority of financiers

124

and corporation leaders who controlled the industrialization of the country. They faced a wrenching dilemma.

Believing in political and social freedom, as well as an open marketplace, their first thought was to support other people who respected those principles. Yet, unable to break out of the ideology and psychology of the marketplace Present toward a cooperative or communitarian Future, they increasingly demanded that others exercise the right of self-determination in ways that furthered the economic expansion of America that they deemed essential for their own self-determination. Their compromise was made easier because the great majority of them also believed in their souls that America had evolved the best ideas and institutions of freedom.[1]

Many of them supported the Cuban revolutionaries during the Ten Years' War from 1868 to 1878, for example, while at the same time talking of the need to guide them into the American Present in order to facilitate the expansion of agricultural exports. That was "in the interest of mankind everywhere." One of their most influential spokesmen revealed the imperialism inherent in their vision as early as 1868: "Our form of government," thundered Ignatius Donnelly of Minnesota, "is adapted to civilized man everywhere. . . . Great as we are, we are yet in the day of small things. . . . Let us, then, while perfecting our institutions, not refuse to expand our boundaries."

Another giant spoke their truth even more forcefully. Henry Demarest Lloyd was an urban reformer who respected his agricultural comrades and sought to build an alliance with them that would be strong enough to improve life for all Americans. But he shared Seward's desire to combine

[1] I have explored the details of this process in *The Roots of the Modern American Empire* (New York, Random House, 1969).

125

mission and uniqueness and expansion. "If nobody can lick us," he remarked in the mid-1880s, "we need not be afraid to play the just and generous big brother among the nations." His rhetoric became a bit more traditional—though no less imperial—during the ensuing decade. "I would extend the Monroe Doctrine," he advised in 1895, "to the assistance of every people seeking to establish the Republic." That was the only way "to fulfill our mission to defend and *extend* liberty."

The Monroe Doctrine was not, however, extended to the freed slaves, the First Americans, the urban workers, or even to female whites. Once unshackled from their chattel chains, the Blacks were tossed into the pit of the marketplace. The effort by abolitionists and others to equip them for the terrors of that kind of freedom was never very impressive, and it soon crumpled under the pressures of indifference—"After all, they's free, ain't they?"—and the fear of them as competitors. They were allowed to slip (and were often shoved) into the servitude of sharecropping and noncitizenship as if the right of self-determination had never existed.

The few First Americans who still survived were hunted down and killed. Well, not all; just most. We did not destroy all the people, we just erased their cultures and swept the survivors out of sight. We did not bother to keep accurate records until those who remained became our wards, so nobody knows how many died. Those who were so concerned about preserving the American Present, including the reformers in Kansas and Chicago, did not count the First Americans as part of America.

As for females, they were largely free to self-determine themselves as housewives, field workers, mistresses, charwomen, cheap labor in the factories, and ladies of the night. The gutsy few who insisted upon more were encouraged, or seduced, to become mother-reformers of America just as America was the reformer of the world. And those rare ones, like the imaginative Charlotte Gilman, who recognized the need to change the *structure* of society—to move it into the Future—were ignored even by the majority of reformers.

The male industrial workers who dared to assert the right of self-determination were fired, hauled through court on the way to jail, or put under the gun. It was a grim time, and many were killed and maimed, or shucked out into limbo. The American Present was marketplace individualism and, while it was wholly acceptable to invoke the word *Union* to glorify that truth, it was subversive to organize a union. People who wanted to self-determine themselves as members of a community were viewed by most as either hankering for the Bad Past or whoring after the Bad Future. Unless, of course, one was a member of the board of directors of a corporation—or a high government official. That kind of self-determination into an elite was honored as the ultimate expression of the unique American mission and the right of self-determination.

## II

Our fingers scrawling on the wall of history thus told first about the decline of self-determination at home, but they soon scratched the story of our empire. The first episode inspired some hope that the victory over the Confederacy might revive the commitment to the principle of self-determination. The French conquest of Mexico in 1863 was a gross (and pathetic) violation of that right; and Seward, as soon as it became possible, exerted strong pressure on Napoleon III to withdraw his puppet king. The Mexicans would undoubtedly have accomplished that objective on their own, but the American assistance hastened their vic-

tory. It was a classic example of the convergence of interest
and principle. America's concern to control the Western
Hemisphere as part of its Present was implemented by supporting Mexican self-determination.

But events in Cuba made it apparent that the determination to preserve the Present enjoyed a higher priority.
The revolution against Spanish colonialism that erupted on
October 10, 1868, was fired by a deep commitment to self-
determination that carried the Cubans through ten years of
war—and was even then not extinguished. Their struggle
immediately evoked widespread sympathy and support
among Americans.

Many whites, for example, as well as Blacks led by
Frederick Douglass, responded enthusiastically to the revolutionary declaration ending slavery on the island. Others
saw another convergence of interest and principle: a free
Cuba would model itself (no doubt with some friendly assistance) upon the United States and open vast markets.
Those concerns for Cuba to become like America, and to
define its Future as part of the American Present, were
clouds arising from the sea that forecast further distortions
of the commitment to self-determination.

As it became clear that the revolutionaries were capable of a sustained effort against Spain, the pressure to
recognize them as belligerents (and thus enable them legally
to buy arms and supplies) became extremely powerful.
President Ulysses Grant was strongly inclined to take such
action, but he allowed himself to be immobilized by a combination of forces. The public agitation, reinforced by the
advice of his close friend Secretary of War John A. Rawlins,
pushed him toward recognition. But Grant was ultimately
cowed by the persistent opposition of Secretary of State
Hamilton Fish.

Fish was a powerful and impressive New Yorker who

spoke for a significant minority which was determined to control Cuba's development after it broke free of Spain. The roots of their attitude went deep into the minds of the Founding Fathers, all of whom would have taken Cuba if they could have done so with impunity. Fish held a low view of most Cubans (and other colored peoples), and argued that it would be unwise to recognize them until they had displayed the proper degree of stability and the competence to organize the island as part of the American Present. And he revealed the kind of commanding arrogance that intimidated Grant on crucial ocasions.

Some of the President's unwillingness to force the issue, however, was grounded in his intense desire to annex Santo Domingo. He was playing his own games with self-determination, and hence lacked a solid base from which to attack and overrule Fish. In the end, therefore, the Cubans were defeated and America gave another twist to the ideal of self-determination.

Others followed quickly. The French Revolution of 1870 produced another radical commune, which provoked a demand to "drive these devils into the sea." The *"red flag"* had been raised by the "rush of the mob," and matters grew "worse from day to day." The Future looked dark indeed, and hence America should extend active support to "the friends of law and order." The French agents of conservatism did quite well, however, without any help from Washington. Representative Richard Jacobs Haldeman of Pennsylvania decried the ruthless suppression of people who displayed such idealism and courage. But he stood almost alone. His resolution expressing "profound regret" about those events—"they have been shot down by scores"—was routinely defeated.

American policy makers revealed more interest in helping to self-determine the natives of the African Congo into the Present. That episode in the long campaign to expand Christian capitalist civilization began with the rather bizarre decision by James Gordon Bennett, Jr., chief executive officer of the New York *Herald,* to send Henry Morton Stanley (a Welshman who thought he was an American) off to Africa to find David Livingstone, the Scottish missionary and explorer who was ostensibly lost in Africa. Stanley was an accomplished adventurer, and he found his man; and then greeted him with a remark that became one of the great clichés of circumstance: "Dr. Livingstone, I presume."

The two of them proceeded through their subsequent explorations to correct some of the gross Western misconceptions about the elementary geography of Africa, and in the process generated imperial visions among various Europeans and Americans. One of those was Henry S. Sanford, a wealthy promoter who had served Lincoln effectively as the American minister to Belgium. King Leopold III of that country later hired him to help establish Belgian claims in Africa. But England, France, and Portugal were also interested in controlling the trade and other wealth of the Congo, and that competition posed a significant challenge.

Sanford and Leopold devised a strategy that proved effective. The King first hired Stanley to negotiate trade treaties with the Africans, and then Sanford moved into the jungle of American politics. His objective was to outflank Britain and the other rivals by persuading the United States to recognize the Belgian claim to the Congo. Sanford succeeded by stressing the vast markets for American surpluses, by encouraging various southerners to think that the Congo could absorb a considerable portion of the troublesome Black population in the United States, and by promising that Belgium would grant "equal rights for Americans and American commerce."

The people of the Congo were not consulted; instead

they were considered cheap labor, as a welcoming committee for American Blacks, and as consumers who would buy surplus American cotton cloth to cover their nakedness and thereby move one step down the road to salvation. It was as if the two small clouds arising out of the sea off Cuba had drifted eastward over Africa and generated a bolt of lightning that illuminated the future. The revolutionary right of self-determination was undergoing a mutation into the right of equal opportunity to preserve the American Present throughout the world.

The necessity of economic expansion and the imperative of fulfilling the nation's unique mission, having been temporarily disrupted by the transition to industrialism, were settling in for a long winter's night. Marines were landed in 1885 to control an insurrection in Panama. Two years later, the United States divided Samoa with Germany and Great Britain. Next came a campaign during 1891–92 to control events in Chile and Peru. Then intervention in Brazil to defeat revolutionaries who opposed economic penetration by American corporations.

And next Hawaii. That episode recalled Texas—with a difference. Led by traders, missionaries, and whalers, Americans had by the 1840s taken effective control of that formerly relaxed kingdom. But the Past remained a constant threat to the American Present. Missionaries married natives and fell away from the gospel into sex and real estate. Traders and whalers left the marketplace and settled down to being merely human. Melville knew all about those warm brown bodies and those happy souls. It posed a dangerous situation for those who viewed Hawaii as a stepping-stone on the way across the Pacific to preserve the American civilization in Asia.

The realists, as they called themselves (even then), took charge. The Americans in Hawaii called in the marines and on January 16, 1893, self-determined themselves as the true Hawaiians. It was a nasty business, and it provoked an angry cry of outrage among those who wanted more freedom in America—and who had tried to help the Cubans. Those people changed their minds, however, when President Grover Cleveland proposed to give some control of Hawaii back to the Hawaiians.

Cleveland was not a crusader, merely a Buffalo businessman with a compass and a ruler who thought that he could square the circle even as he projected the American marketplace into infinity. The United States, he argued, could honor its commitment to self-determination and simultaneously use Hawaii as a springboard to the markets of Asia. All those good things could be accomplished by giving Queen Liliuokalani the trappings of power while retaining the substance of control. But she was a tough Hawaiian who replied in essence: we will accept at face value your avowed respect for our independence, and in return will allow you to use our finest harbor, but we insist upon our right to control the essentials of our lives.

Fair enough, but not enough for Americans. The loudest *NOs* came from the prairie reformers, people who advocated freedom as long as it preserved the American Present. They wanted the freedom of a free marketplace; but when the choice came, they chose markets. They considered it an abomination to give Hawaii back to Queen Lil. "It seems ridiculous," cried one in a typical response, "to suppose that the United States Government ever contemplated the use of force for the purpose of restoring a monarchy."

# III

And so another step toward global empire, the final projection of Lincoln's rewriting of the right of self-determination. If you can kill your brother (or your neighbor) in the name of preserving your Present, then you can kill anyone to preserve your Present. And will. Consider the Cubans and the Filipinos. The Cubans reopened their revolution against Spain on February 24, 1895, and again evoked widespread sympathy in the United States. But this time there were few Americans who denied—or damned—the twisted relationship between the desire to support the Cubans and the determination to preserve the American Present, and the concern to honor the principle of self-determination.

Almost everyone defined a free Cuba as a Cuba integrated into the American marketplace system. In the end that meant war, and a policy of overriding Cuban revolutionaries in favor of Cubans who were willing to accept the American Present. President William McKinley was simple and direct about it all: the rebels would not be allowed to determine either the Present or the Future of Cuba. They were not even permitted to participate in the parade that celebrated the defeat of Spain.

The Filipinos, who had been freed from Spain even before the Cubans, chose to fight a war against that narrow definition of self-determination accepted in Washington. Their courage upset many Americans. But in the end, the majority decided that the Philippines were necessary to preserve the American way of life. Manila, they agreed, was vital to carrying civilization into China, and Manila could not be controlled unless the entire archipelago was occupied to prepare it as part of the Global Commonwealth.

It was a beastly war. Water torture was the least of it. People destroyed each other in every way they could devise. Honest men lost their souls even though they were not killed. People were still killing each other as late as 1902, by which time the United States had again helped to repress an outbreak of self-determination in China.

The process of opening Asia to Western power and

influence, which began early in the nineteenth century, initially involved a forceful abridgement of Chinese self-determination in controlling opium and other economic artifacts offered for sale by westerners. Some Americans recognized that truth from the outset. "China has a perfect right," one of them pointed out in 1843, "to regulate the character of her imports." But most of the people who were involved interpreted the Chinese and Japanese desire to remain aloof from the West as an infringement upon the American right of self-determination, and as an example of the Bad Past blocking the progress of the Good Christian and capitalist Present.

Though they were not actively engaged in the fighting, American naval vessels did contribute to the more general show of force during the British war against China (1839–41) that broached China's defenses. The United States then took the offensive against Japan. The penetration of China provided the setting for the arrival of Commodore Matthew C. Perry's fleet in Tokyo Bay in 1853–54, and he added his own touch of terror by painting his ships black. It was all most effective.

The United States was simultaneously throwing its weight against revolutionaries in China. Led by Hung Siutshuen, the forces of the Taiping Rebellion captured Nanking in 1853 and established themselves as the rulers of the Yangtze Valley. Some Americans argued for a policy of supporting Hung, seeing more to be gained by breaking down the Bad Past. "That is where to introduce the wedge, where to rest the lever." But Humphrey Marshall, the American commissioner, thought it would be wiser to support the existing system. That would prevent England and other countries from carving China into colonies, and at the same time open the way for the United States to take the lead in "maintaining order here, and gradually engrafting on this worn-out stock the healthy principles" of the Present.

That view prevailed. The revolution was suppressed, and America embarked upon a policy of supporting various parties of law and order. The objective was to create a China too weak to resist the demands of the United States and other Western powers but strong enough to carry out the directions of the civilized powers and control any revolutionaries who wanted to reassert Chinese sovereignty. China would be allowed to self-determine itself into—but not beyond—the American Present.

Seward sustained that policy after the suppression of the Confederate Revolution, and attempted (without much success) to extend it to Korea. By the end of the century, however, as strong secular pressures for expansion strengthened the missionary urge to lead China out of the wilderness, the policy was challenged by Japan as well as by European powers and by a militant nationalist movement in China.

American leaders responded, between 1898 and 1900, with a strategy designed to create what they called "an open field with no favor." The object was to block the colonial partition of countries like China and to penetrate existing colonies, thereby enabling American economic power and political influence to control the development of those countries. As finally formulated during 1899 and 1900 in three diplomatic dispatches that came to be called the Open Door Notes, American leaders used the rhetoric of self-determination to mask a policy of sophisticated imperialism. They advanced three points that, taken together, created a system designed to preserve the American Present against both the colonial Past and a revolutionary Future.

First, the United States insisted upon "perfect equality of treatment for their commerce and navigation" throughout China, including those areas then heavily influenced by another power. Second, it announced its determination to play a major role in bringing "permanent safety and peace to China" and in preserving that nation's "territorial and

WILLIAM APPLEMAN WILLIAMS

administrative" integrity. And third, it acknowledged its willingness to help suppress Chinese rebellions or revolutions ("such disasters") that threatened the influence of the civilizing powers.

Theodore Roosevelt later remarked that he considered the Open Door Policy a mere extension of the Monroe Doctrine to Asia and the rest of the world. And Woodrow Wilson subsequently spoke of his own policy in precisely those terms. Those were not casual or rhetorical comparisons, for the essential purpose of the Policy was to establish limits designed to preserve the American way of life.

The United States dramatized its commitment to that Policy in 1900 by sending a sizable military force to China. The dual purpose was to help repress the Chinese uprising known as the Boxer Rebellion and to make it clear to Russia, Japan, and other nations that Washington was serious about keeping China open to American power and influence. The great importance attached to the action was revealed most dramatically by the decision to expedite the deployment of troops in China by withdrawing them from the Philippines even before the revolutionary forces in that country had been crushed.

## IV

Combined with the related actions in Cuba and the Philippines, the formulation of the Open Door Policy and the counterrevolutionary intervention in China served to clarify and establish an American policy that remained essentially unchanged into our own time. It is useful, therefore, to review the relationship of that policy to the primary elements of the original American *Weltanschauung*.

First, the Open Door Policy sustained the traditional

belief that economic and political expansion was necessary. The earlier emphasis on acquiring contiguous agricultural land was modified to meet the needs of a capitalist industrial system for markets and raw materials, but the willingness to add more territory did not disappear. Americans continued to establish their control over various pieces of real estate that they considered essential to preserving the Present.

Such action was often advocated or justified with strategic arguments about national security; but military logic about security is based upon, and is derived from, the initial assumptions about what is to be protected. A nonimperial America, for example, would feel no necessity to *attack* (let alone *possess*) the Philippines, no need to establish economic and political predominance *within* Cuba and other countries, and no imperative to build bases around the world.

Second, the Civil War and the subsequent victories over the First Americans, Cubans, and Filipinos, along with the rapid industrialization of the country, reinforced other elements of the *Weltanschauung*. Americans viewed themselves as a people rapidly becoming the most powerful nation in the world, and that sense of being alone at the top strengthened the feelings of isolation and uniqueness. And the possession of such power underscored the missionary duty to expand the area of freedom. The Open Door Policy brought them all together in its assumption that American economic supremacy would control the development of China (and other nations), and in its stand against European colonialism.

Third, the commitment to self-determination emerged from the events at the end of the century in a highly qualified form. The United States continued to use the rhetoric of self-determination to define its policy, but in practice it increasingly hedged the principle. The only vestige of the original ideal was a continuing willingness to support self-determination into the American Present.

But even that was weakened by the propensity to favor proponents of the Past if they proved willing to accommodate themselves to American expansion, and by a growing tendency to interfere in other countries to insure that the process of self-determination proceeded in accordance with American conceptions of civilization. And it shortly became apparent that the United States would intervene vigorously against any society that sought to self-determine itself into the Future.

# 8

# Woodrow Wilson
# and the Second Crusade
# to Save the Present

Any country whose people conduct themselves well
can count upon our hearty friendship. If a nation shows
that it knows how to act with reasonable efficiency
and decency in social and political matters, if it keeps
order and pays its obligations, it need fear no
interference from the United States. Chronic
wrongdoing, or an impotence which results in a general
loosening of the ties of civilized society, may in
America . . . force the United States, however
reluctantly, in flagrant cases of such wrongdoing or
impotence, to the exercise of an international police
power.

> —Theodore Roosevelt, 1904

I am going to teach the South American republics to
elect good men!

> —Woodrow Wilson, 1914

The world must be made safe for democracy.

> —Woodrow Wilson, 1917

The first concerted effort to organize the world according to the Open Door Policy was undertaken by President Woodrow Wilson. It was a crusade that William Bolitho [Ryall] aptly included in his study of *Twelve Against the Gods*. For Wilson, the historian become President, was proposing nothing less than the conquest of Time and Change. He aspired to make "the world safe for democracy," by which he meant making it safe for the American Present. He would do for the world what Lincoln had done for America. Thus it is necessary, while acknowledging the impressive nature of the proposal, to keep in mind that it involved a fundamental distortion of the commitment to self-determination that began with counterrevolutionary intervention in Mexico, and ended in similar action in Russia.

# I

Wilson's crusade is usually associated with American entry into the First World War; but his early historical writings and his conduct of foreign affairs prior to 1917 make it clear that he had been thinking in such terms for many years. As he worked his way to the White House, moreover, his rival Theodore Roosevelt was laying down the general guidelines, experimenting with various strategies and tactics, and establishing important precedents.

Wilson was highly susceptible to severe attacks of moralistic sermonizing, but Roosevelt prided himself as a realist. And TR *had* emerged from his aristocratic association with Brooks Adams and others with a propensity to think and talk in the no-nonsense idiom of empire. He agreed with Adams, Turner, and Mahan on the central theme of expansion in American history, and so argued that the country must build and be prepared to use a mighty military force. Roosevelt had charged San Juan Hill to help bring Cuba into the American Present, and subsequently used the navy to underscore the American presence around the world.

But just as Wilson revealed a deep concern for economic expansion and a ruthless willingness to use force, so Roosevelt preached the uniqueness and mission of the United States. He favored the apocalyptic language of civilization and decay, and in his first major address as President spoke bluntly about the necessity of military intervention to discipline "barbarous or semibarbarous peoples." Such actions involved no major danger; they were "merely a most regrettable but necessary international police duty which must be performed for the welfare of mankind."

After that overture, Roosevelt moved into his first act: pushing Colombia down the road toward civilization. His intervention to transform its northern province into the nation of Panama, and thereby acquire the territory and the power to build an American canal linking the Atlantic and the Pacific, was an arrogant violation of the principle of self-determination. The Panamanians had long sought more autonomy (or independence), but Roosevelt demeaned their honest struggle and left them still dreaming about freedom.

He next generalized that approach to all Latin American countries. Their economic domination by the United States and other industrial countries trapped them in a vicious circle of international debt and domestic despotism. Intervention by the United States was considered to be civilizing, but similar action by European powers was viewed as a threat to the American Present. A thoughtful Argentine official named Luis Maria Drago offered in 1902 a proposal that was designed to break out of the box. While accepting

141

the ideal of a Hemispheric System, and the reality of American predominance, Drago sought to build a more equitable relationship which would give the Latin American nations more independence.

He suggested that *all* countries in the Western Hemisphere stand together against European interventions. Most of those actions grew out of economic claims, and hence the solution was simple: present a united front against their interference and work out a plan to meet the financial obligations owed to foreign nations. Roosevelt would have nothing to do with that kind of proposal. It not only exposed the United States to the possibility of being outvoted by semibarbarous people, but neither he nor any other American leader was prepared to limit his self-determined right of intervention. That was opening a door into a Future that they had no intention of entering.

Roosevelt replied to Drago on December 6, 1904, with a sweeping assertion of the right and the intention of the United States to control the self-determination of all countries in the Western Hemisphere within the limits of the American Present. After again reciting the catechism about not desiring any more territory, he made it clear that only those people who "conduct themselves well can count upon our hearty friendship." The standards of behavior were strictly those of the United States. Any country that "knows how to act with reasonable efficiency and decency in social and political matters," and "keeps order and pays its obligations," would have nothing to worry about.

But "wrongdoing or impotence" will require the United States to exercise its self-determined "international police power." "Obey the primary laws of civilized society," Roosevelt said, and you have nothing to fear. But if you fail to make "good use" of your right to independence you can expect the United States to intervene "in our own interest as well as in the interest of humanity at large."

Roosevelt then turned to Africa, where preserving the American Present took the form of cooperating with Europeans to control the natives and prepare them for civilization. Displaying a keen understanding of long-range strategy that was unquestionably informed by his discussions with Secretary of State Elihu Root, the President concentrated on two objectives. First, to prevent a war among the civilizing nations of Europe, in this case Germany, France, and England, for that would risk the destruction of the Present. Second, to establish ground rules and procedures for guiding the Past (*including* European colonialism) into the civilized world of the Open Door System. Secretary Root described it all in one of the classic dispatches of American diplomatic history.

At the heart of the process, Root began, was "security of life and property." Then it was necessary to establish "equality of opportunities for trade with all natives; amelioration of those domestic conditions of religion and class which now weigh upon non-Musselmans, and which impair the freedom of salutary foreign intercourse with the native population; improvement of the condition of the people that will enable them to profit by the opportunities of foreign traffic; orderly and certain administration of impartial justice; rigorous punishment of crimes against persons and property; exemption from erratic taxes and burdens; removal of class restrictions; and the power to repress subversive disorder and preserve the public peace."

All those conditions were essential to "policing the interior and . . . removing the barriers which have heretofore opposed the foreigner at the threshold and the non-Musselman in the interior. In short, while it is to the advantage of the powers to secure the 'open door' it is equally vital to their interests and no less so to the advantage of Morocco that the door, being open, shall lead to something; that the outside world shall benefit by assured op-

WILLIAM APPLEMAN WILLIAMS

portunities, and that the Moroccan people shall be made in a measure fit and able to profit by the advantages of the proposed reform."

## II

Though written for a specific purpose, Root's candid description of how the Open Door Policy inherently restricted the self-determination of other countries also provided a striking preview of subsequent developments during the Wilson era. For, whatever their other differences, Roosevelt and Wilson strutted to the same drummer in foreign policy. Both were historians who had been strongly influenced by Frederick Jackson Turner's frontier thesis. America needed to expand and therefore would expand. The alternatives were old despotism or new anarchy. "If America is not to have free enterprise," asserted Wilson, "then she can have freedom of no sort whatever." And capitalism was dependent upon expansion. "Our industries have expanded to such a point that they will burst their jackets if they cannot find a free outlet to the markets of the world." As for limits, "Who shall say where it will end?"

But Wilson was also idealistic. America was destined to be "the justest, the most progressive, the most honorable, the most enlightened Nation in the world." His first Secretary of State, William Jennings Bryan, agreed: American power was a God-given benediction to be used to "prevent revolutions, promote education, and advance stable and just government." Bryan was proud to be associated with a President who had "opened the doors of all the weaker countries to an invasion of American capital and American enterprise." It was the work of the Lord. And the marines, those instruments of "the Good Samaritan" whom Bryan called to duty to control the forces of evil in the Caribbean.

144

As for Wilson, he considered the philosophy of revolution "radically evil and corrupting." "Revolutions always put things back and sensible reforms are postponed." The "slow process of reform" was the only true faith, and America had a sacred obligation to sustain and extend that gospel throughout the world—using force as it proved necessary. The true way was to use American power to insure "the slow and steady improvement of mankind through the spread of a reformed and socially responsible democratic capitalism." Wilson would approve and recognize only "those who act in the interest of peace and honor, who protect private rights, and respect the restraints of constitutional procedures."

"I will not cry 'peace,'" he avowed, "as long as there is sin and wrong in the world." That made for busy days—and nights—in the White House. He began in China and Mexico. The Chinese revolution that erupted in October, 1911, posed a challenge and an opportunity for American policy makers. The conservative faction led by Yüan Shih-k'ai offered a traditional program of law and order which promised to facilitate the extension of American influence. The liberal and radical groups that rallied around Sun Yat-sen held out the prospect of a modernized China becoming an equal among nations. Wilson recognized Yüan and cried peace as that military leader purged and then dissolved the Chinese parliament. A good day's work for the Open Door and the cause, as Wilson expressed it, of helping China by expanding "the standards of the West."

The Mexicans, however, were not in the mood for being self-determined by the scholar in the White House. They fought gallantly for their vision of the Future. And in the process revealed that the American commitment to the revolutionary right of self-determination was being eased into the Bad Past. The details are dreary and depressing and accumulate like guano to a conclusion that is nicely stated by Wilson's sympathetic biographer, Arthur K. Link: the President was determined "to shape the Mexican Revolution into a constitutional and moralistic pattern of his own making." Or, as Wilson phrased it: "I am going to teach the South American republics to elect good men!"

The President attempted political seduction, tried chicanery, manipulated food and arms in ways that killed unnumbered Mexicans, and intervened with force. The Mexicans displayed great courage and ultimately (along with the Russians and the Chinese) forced Wilson and other Americans to confront the reality of the Future. All those peoples were saying, each in its own way, that the American Present was not their preference as a way of life, and that it was most certainly not going to last forever.

In the course of dealing with that challenge, Wilson had to cope with a Japanese effort to force China into its own version of the Present. They had mastered Commodore Perry's lesson and hence saw themselves as the Americans of Asia: they would help all the people of Asia to self-determine themselves as moral and efficient Japanese. It was as though the torch of uniqueness and mission had been passed from Boston and Virginia to Tokyo. Louisiana had become Manchuria: a desirable and necessary extension of the Present, and a golden opportunity to bring backward peoples into the civilized Present.

Wilson did not view it in those exact terms, but he and many others did think of Japan as America's younger brother and helpmate in the Far East. The Chinese and the Russians (like the Mexicans) were fascinating people, but too inclined to honor the Past, and even to consider it as a source of ideas for the Future. So the President temporized in 1915 when Japan exerted strong pressure on China. Too far, too fast, he cautioned: keep Korea and Manchuria, but

146

we must work together carefully throughout the rest of China. Trying to force the Present will open the way for the forces of sin and revolution. And, of course, Japan must always remember that the United States will insist upon its right to play a major role in the process. Not surprisingly, Wilson approached and dealt with the confrontation as part of what he considered a grand effort to extend and maintain "the policy of the open door to the world."

## III

The attempt to fulfill that pretentious ambition led rapidly to a long series of military interventions. First in Haiti, where the marines landed in 1915 and established a protectorate after squashing all revolutionary activity. Then again in Mexico. Wilson's determination to control that revolution led him to support Francisco Villa against Venustiano Carranza, even though the latter was leading a social revolution that generated increasing enthusiasm and attracted growing support throughout Mexico.

Wilson threatened to intervene directly but soon realized that such action would entail a massive war against the Mexican people. As Carranza moved ever closer to success, Villa began raiding American centers in northern Mexico and along the border in the hope of provoking American action. The ploy proved effective, and in March, 1916, Wilson moved a large force into Mexico ostensibly to capture Villa. That violated both the spirit and the letter of the reluctant authorization granted by Carranza for a small force, aroused intense anger among Mexicans, and created a serious crisis.

Strong domestic opposition to such a war, exerted by individuals and such organizations as the American Union Against Militarism, played a vital role in averting a catastrophe. Wilson did not want a war, but his determination to control the Mexican revolution had carried him to the threshold of such a conflict. At the same time, the President was also deeply concerned to exercise American power in Europe, and that consideration, along with Carranza's firmness and the pro-Mexican sentiment, preserved the peace.

The public's reassertion of the American commitment to the right of self-determination proved an ironic victory, however, for Wilson shortly took the nation into a much larger war in the name of self-determination. And though a significant number of people opposed that action, a majority enthusiastically supported the crusade to "make the world safe for democracy."

Wilson was in the short run concerned with Imperial Germany. He viewed it as a major economic and political threat to the Open Door System and as the Past rising in renewed power to challenge the Present. That involved a specter that could not be allowed the right of self-determination. But the President was also deeply worried about the behavior of England, France, and Japan, and by the possibility that the war, if it was not stopped soon, would open the door for unknown dangers.

The only way to preserve the American Present was to organize the world according to American principles. Wilson revealed that purpose in a January, 1917, speech to the Senate, announcing bluntly at the outset that it was "inconceivable" that the United States would not be involved in the settlement of the war. That was, he explained, "the opportunity for which [Americans] have sought to prepare themselves by the very principles and purposes of their polity and the approved practices of their Government ever since the days when they set up a new nation in the high and honorable hope that it might in all that it was and did show mankind the way to liberty." Then, after a strong assertion of the right of self-determination, he reiterated the essentials of the Open Door Policy and suggested that the Monroe Doctrine be extended from the Western Hemisphere to the globe.

"These are American principles, American policies," Wilson accurately noted. "We could stand for no others." Then, in a starkly revealing passage, he defined good people as those who accepted the American Present. "And they are also the principles and policies of forward-looking men and women everywhere, or every modern nation, of every enlightened community. They are the principles of mankind and must prevail."

One year later, after America had entered the war, Wilson restated and amplified those themes in his more famous Fourteen Points speech. He also underscored his missionary determination. "The program of the world's peace, therefore, is our program . . . the only possible program, as we see it." By that time, however, the American Present was being challenged by the Future as well as the Past.

The Mexican Constitution of 1917 drew upon that culture's great traditions to reassert the principle of communal property against the possessive individualism of the imperial marketplace. The continuing ferment in China revealed that it, too, was determined to self-determine itself in a non-American pattern. But the most shattering news came from Russia. The Bolsheviks who seized power in that country on November 7, 1917, were proudly and defiantly committed to the vision of the Future that Karl Marx had offered in 1848. The Past was threatening to become the Future.

## IV

To say that those revolutions represented the Future is not to assert that they were or became the embodiment of all things good and true. I do not think that any of them created Heaven from our mortal clay; although I do think all of them offer alternatives which are worth adapting to our own culture. But to say that they were Future-oriented is to insist upon several other things that are at least as important—and for us Americans very probably more important.

First, they were major social revolutions that we must respect if we are to honor our central commitment to the right of self-determination. When a society is afraid of fundamental change, and that fear pervades America, it usually makes much use of the argument that revolutions are the work of a minority which does not represent the majority. The proposition is a classic half-truth. Revolutions are always made by a minority: think only of our break with Great Britain; of the movement that created the Constitution; and of the southern secessionists. But those minorities do not sustain themselves unless they evoke general support or acquiescence. It is no answer to say that all those revolutions involved violence, for that is an inherent part of great social upheavals. Consider only the violence of the American Revolution, and the subsequent suppression of the First Americans, and the Confederate Revolution.

Second, all those revolutions looked beyond the Present as defined by the possessive individualism of Western capitalism. They were motivated by the vision of a more just and equitable way to live together as human beings. We can easily lose sight of that truth, for we are the victims of the calculated schizophrenia we practice in order to retain some measure of sanity in an irrational society.

We tell ourselves, on the one hand, that the corporation and the welfare state have transcended possessive individualism. But, on the other hand, we know that the corporation and the federal bureaucracy are even more possessive than the old individual capitalists—and also that

150

we have settled for possessing *things* as our substitute for meaningful participation in making a better life. Hence in the end we are inclined to view all communal institutions as corporations and so dismiss and damn those who struggle to create a community which will supercede the corporation.

Third, all people who develop a sense of the Future draw upon their knowledge and feeling for the Past. Americans sense that truth but remain deeply fearful of its demands and implications.[1] I am not talking in a narrow sense about what is called "a usable past": old ideas or policies that may be relevant to present problems. I am speaking instead of the knowing in the soul that tells us of our primary nature as a culture; of what in our identity and experience is good and what is bad, and of how to use the good to overcome a bit more of the bad. But that kind of confrontation with ourselves inherently changes the present in vital and fundamental ways; and so Wilson, and countless others, talked instead about the dangers of anarchy and despotism, and socialism and communism. There are dangers there, but not the ones we Americans have emphasized.

Fourth, our commitment to the right of revolutionary self-determination demands that we allow other people to make their mistakes just as we demand the right to make ours—and attempt to realize their visions just as we have struggled to preserve the Present.

But Wilson, like Lincoln, was afraid of the Future. And so in the end he did not respect the tradition. Instead he used it to preserve the Present and dishonored it to block the Future. He supported safe states in Europe, ignored Sun Yat-sen in China and Black leaders in Africa (and America), sent marines to the Caribbean, and maintained his hostility toward Mexico.

He understood the issue, so to respect him is to make

[1] This fear of the Past is an essential element of American anti-intellectualism, a relationship that may have already been seen by many readers.

**151**

no excuses for him. He simply flunked the course. He said in January, 1918, that the "acid test" was the treatment of Russia: how the United States dealt with the Future as socialism or communism. He aborted it in Hungary and tried to destroy it in Russia. And crushed it in America.

Its leader, Eugene Debs, entered the turmoil of the 1890s as a militant but orthodox labor leader and emerged as a charismatic Socialist. He was an uncommon radical who evoked a widespread response among farmers as well as factory workers, among women as well as men—indeed, among all groups in all parts of the country. He viewed the American Past an an honorable childhood in preparation for a Socialist adulthood. Wilson threw him in jail because he opposed entering the war and refused him a pardon even after the armistice. The President likewise employed the vast powers of the government to squash the Socialist movement.

But Wilson failed to accomplish all his self-appointed tasks. He was unable to institutionalize the American Present in the League of Nations, and he had to settle for less than he wanted in Mexico, China, and Russia. He made the mistake that he had warned the Japanese to avoid: he went too far, too fast, and for a moment he revived the tradition of the commitment to self-determination among enough Americans to insure his defeat.

# 9
## A Moment of Reflection and Rededication

[The] flowering [of pragmatism] appears in the technical organization of the war by an earnest group of young liberals, who direct their course by an opportunist programme of State-socialism at home and a league of benevolently imperialistic nations abroad.

—Randolph Bourne, 1917

I want for my part to go in and accept what is offered us, the leadership of the world.

—Woodrow Wilson, 1919

There was throughout the world a feeling of revolt against the large vested interests which influenced the world both in the economic and in the political sphere. The way to cure this domination was, in [my] opinion, constant discussion and a slow process of reform; but the world at large had grown impatient of delay.

—Woodrow Wilson, 1919

You must either give them independence, recognize
their rights as nations to live their own life and to set
up their own form of government, or you must deny
them those things by force.
—Senator William E. Borah of Idaho, 1919

A large part of the world has come to believe that
they were in the presence of the birth of a new imperial
power intent upon dominating the destinies and
freedoms of other peoples.
—Herbert Hoover, 1927

Even the more defensible aspects of Wilson's program
and action, such as the creation of ethnically defined national states and his effort to ameliorate some aspects of
colonial rule, could not mask the contradiction inherent in
the attempt to impose the American Present upon the world
in the name of self-determination. The reaction against that
crusade, which actually began as the President was moving
toward intervention in the war, led many people into serious
reflection about the central importance of the principle of
self-determination in the American *Weltanschauung*. That
thought, and the related rededication to the principle, influenced policy in a significant way for more than a decade.

That is hardly a moment in historical time, and it was
all but forgotten in the subsequent crusade against the revolutions that challenged the American Present in the name
of the Future. But it was an important moment, and it is
a part of our Past that can help us in creating our own
Future.

# I

Some Americans, conservatives and liberals as well
as radicals, had always understood the vital significance of

the commitment to the right of revolutionary self-determination and had struggled to honor it as it became distorted in the name of preserving the Present. The Quakers, the advocates of a live-and-let-live policy toward the First Americans, those who opposed the war of conquest against Mexico, and the northerners who argued for allowing the Confederacy to go its way in peace were the most notable examples during the first part of our history.

Then came the tiny group of true anti-imperialists which fought against the extension of the continental empire into Hawaii, Cuba, the Philippines, and China. And, finally, those who resisted another war against Mexico and those who rejected the idea of turning the war against Germany into a global crusade. Two of that latter group, Senators Robert M. La Follette and William E. Borah, did much to carry the battle on into the postwar era.

After a youthful fling with imperialism during the era of the Spanish-American War, La Follette became increasingly critical of expansionist ideas and policies. He respected Wilson's efforts at domestic reform (though he considered them insufficient), but differed sharply on foreign policy issues. His strong disagreement over intervention in Mexico was part of a growing resistance to all such activities in Latin America.

La Follette's opposition to American involvement in World War I was gravely misunderstood at the time and caused him great personal and political trouble. He acknowledged that the United States had serious practical grievances against Germany and supported most war measures after the decision was made. But he felt that Wilson's approach involved the strong probability that America would become enmeshed in "years of war" and "imperialism and exploitation." Thus he joined Borah and others to terminate Wilson's intervention against the Bolshevik Revolution and to defeat his effort to define the United States as the dominating power in the League of Nations.

Unlike La Follette, Borah had accepted the necessity of war against Germany, but he did share his colleague's reservations about Wilson's grandiose plans to save the world for the American Present. "I join no crusade," Senator Borah warned bluntly in 1917, and honored that commitment. Wilson's proposal reminded him of the history of the Holy Alliance. The project might start with lofty rhetoric about high Christian principles, but it would shortly degenerate into an alliance against everyone who wanted to change the *status quo*.

"The proposition," Borah concluded, "is force to destroy force, conflict to prevent conflict, militarism to destroy militarism, and war to prevent war." Put simply, the United States would become "a party to the rule of force." That would be a flagrant violation of America's fundamental duty to honor the principle of self-determination. "You must either give them independence, recognize their rights as nations to live their own life and to set up their own form of government, or you must deny them those things by force."

Wilson candidly (and happily) admitted that his plan would give America "the leadership of the world" but insisted that it would be "a liberating power." And he implied that the moral and military power of the United States would deter any future attempts to challenge the liberator. Thorstein Veblen, a witty and scathing critic of American corporation capitalism, replied that the President had done nothing more than to "reinstate the *status quo ante*," and that any effort to preserve it would require interventions unto the end of Time.

And Randolph Bourne, a deeply patriotic radical, viewed it as The Twilight of the Gods—and wept for America. "Men cannot live by politics alone, and it is small cheer that our best intellects . . . see only the hope that America will find her soul in the remaking of the world." Bourne began as a dedicated disciple of John Dewey but came to realize that pragmatism was merely a philosophic rationalization for the Present. Dewey had as little sympathy with revolution as Wilson and identified himself wholly with the President's grand crusade.

Bourne broke free long before that time: he would have none of that sophisticated effort to preserve the Present. Pragmatism had trained its followers "for the executive ordering of events" and left them "pitifully unprepared for the intellectual interpretation or the idealistic focusing of ends." Americans had thus been beguiled into resting "content with getting somewhere without asking too closely whether it was a desirable place to get." America was all technique and no vision. And, Bourne added, "An intellectual attitude of mere adjustment, of mere use of the creative intelligence to make your progress, must end in caution, regression, and a virtual failure to effect even that change which you so clear-sightedly and desirously see." "You never transcend anything. You grow, but your spirit never jumps out of your skin to go on wild adventures. . . ."

But it was not merely reformers and radicals who were appalled by Wilson's program. One of the most devastating criticisms came from Elihu Root, who had earlier offered perhaps the most illuminating analysis of how the Open Door System should be operated to bring the Past into the Present. The President's peace treaty, he caustically commented, represented "an attempt to preserve for all time unchanged the distribution of power and territory made . . . in this present juncture of affairs. . . . It would not only be futile; it would be mischievous. Change and growth are the law of life, and no generation can impose its will in regard to the growth of nations and the distributions of power upon succeeding generations."

Root was not so much changing his outlook as he was arguing the necessity of the very pragmatic adaptation that Bourne deplored. Wilson was too doctrinaire and inflexible. He failed to recognize the elemental force of self-determination and so thought he could control it once and forever. Root was more perceptive, more intelligently conservative, than the President: he understood—from a different perspective—Bourne's central insight; the way to preserve the American Present was to avoid *any* vision. We want to project the present into all tomorrows, Root was saying, so do not play God and assume that every detail has to stay the same. Concentrate on preserving the essentials.

That kind of sophisticated pragmatism guided a significant number of American leaders during the years after the war. Some of them, like Bernard Baruch, stressed the lesson they had learned from World War I and the Bolsheviks. Intervention and war opened the way for revolutions oriented toward the Future. Hence avoid war. Others, like Dwight Morrow of the House of Morgan, were confident in their conservative view of human nature. They did not believe in the existence of the Future. No one could change the world except God, and he was otherwise occupied. Hence all revolutionaries and all revolutions were passing phenomena. Troublesome, perhaps, but not traumatic. Treat them decently, work out pragmatic compromises, and the Future would soon reappear as the Present.

Morrow was an impressive and influential person, but his friend Herbert Clark Hoover was the most intriguing and challenging figure who helped to shape American policy during those years. He was, to risk a quibble about terminology, a conservative with both a sense and a vision of the Future.[1]

[1] The long argument about how to make sense of Hoover has hopefully been terminated by Joan Hoff Wilson, *Herbert Hoover: Forgotten Progressive* (Boston, Little, Brown, 1975).

To know Hoover is to understand what I mean about a sense of the Past, for at times he gives one the eerie feeling that John Quincy Adams was again abroad in the land.

Hoover was a Quaker who tried, in public as well as in private, to honor his faith. His central commitments were to self-determination and to cooperation with other equals as members of a community. He considered the Bill of Rights to be "the heart of the Constitution," and opposed the use of force except in self-defense. Hence he "absolutely disapproved" of global crusades, and made it clear that Dollar Diplomacy was "not a part of my conception of international relations."

He also developed a sense of the Past, and of process, and this enabled him to understand that the possessive individualism of the capitalist marketplace would give way to some other principle of organization and action. Indeed, that change was already under way, and so it was vital to direct it in accordance with humane values. His preference was to revive the concept and practice of active citizenship which would lead people to come together in cooperative ventures to build a better America.

Hoover was in truth offering a limited vision of the Future. It involved a kind of guild capitalism in which the corporation would be balanced (and thereby controlled) by cooperative action among and between farmers, workers, and others.[2] When it became necessary, all people acting as citizens would use the government to acquire assistance, and

[2] Two asides at this point. First, one cannot help wondering if Hoover was influenced by Veblen. Second, there is a great temptation to see Hoover as the precursor of John Kenneth Galbraith, who became famous after 1945 as a liberal pundit who developed an ostensibly original theory about countervailing power within the American Present. And that brings to mind one of Marx's great perceptions into the relationship between the Past and the Present: all things happen twice, once seriously and once as farce. By which I mean that the idea of countervailing power made some sense in the 1920s, but not in the 1950s and 1960s.

to arbitrate conflicts that seemed to have reached an impasse. While it was a contradictory conception in that it accepted certain essentials of the capitalist ethos (as well as the marketplace definition of reality), it was nevertheless a vision of the Future in that it called upon all Americans to assert their right of self-determination to transcend the Present in a way that honored their principles—and their nature as human beings.

If they did not, Hoover continued, the process of change would inexorably produce one of three alternative Futures: socialism, fascism, or a kind of aimless, pragmatic State Syndicalism which would become a bureaucratic nightmare. He thought that America was moving toward the latter fate, and feared that, when it failed, most people would turn "toward Fascism." And he felt strongly that an imperial, crusading foreign policy acted as a powerful force pushing the country toward that terrible demise.

Hoover likewise believed that Future-oriented revolutions, as typified by the Bolsheviks in Russia, were misguided and doomed to failure. But he did understand that they emerged inevitably out of the inequities of the Present and the lack of alternate visions of the Future. He warned Wilson, for example, that massive intervention against such revolutions would "make us party to establishing the reactionary classes in their economic domination over the lower classes." "We shall never remedy justifiable discontent until we eradicate the misery." Force was irrelevant: "We cannot slay an idea or an ideology with machine guns. Ideas live in men's minds in spite of military defeat."

So there we have it: a man with a sense of the Past giving us an eerie preview of the Future. Herbert Hoover and Thorstein Veblen, Randolph Bourne and Wild Bill Borah, and Fighting Bob La Follette and suave Dwight Morrow: strange bedfellows, as the saying goes; and even more exotic than the cliché can encompass because they were united by fidelity to a principle far more than by any common vision of the Future. And they are only the most obvious examples. They were strongly supported, and often advised and influenced, by millions of others who were weary of crusades to save the Present. And by thousands of others who wanted to honor the principle of self-determination— at home as well as abroad.

Consider, for example, William B. Du Bois. The intellectual peer of any white leader, and superior to most, who fought Wilson's deep racial prejudices as they affected domestic and foreign policy. A man with a vision of a communitarian future, and the courage to honor it unto death. Or think of Raymond Robins, an open and zestful man who thought his way into the Future. He began as a dedicated supporter of Theodore Roosevelt and ended as a democratic socialist. Or Charles Austin Beard, a vital, sparkling scholar who insisted that the purpose of a knowledge of the Past was to help (and incite) us to imagine and create a more humane Future. He, too, was willing to take the risk of self-determining America.

And all the others who never are mentioned in history books. The thousands of females who made the Women's League for Peace and Freedom into an effective voice for sanity. The ministers, and the members of their parishes, who revived the old idea that to be a Christian means to help people find their own way unto the Lord. Yes, and all the radicals—Socialists and Communists and others— who every day did the chores that helped the poor and the Black and the old survive the American Present through their faith in a vision of a better future.

All those people were vitally important in recalling and honoring the commitment to the principle of self-determination. They were the power which forced President Calvin Coolidge to send Morrow to Mexico to negotiate the issues of oil and land, and that led to a compromise which gave the Mexicans a chance to make at least some decisions on the basis of their own preferences. They were the people who supported China's claim to equality with other nations. And the ones who backed Hoover's determination to end American intervention in Latin America and his refusal to embark upon another crusade to save the American Present in Asia.

Hoover was not merely concerned to bring the marines home to their lovers, wives, and families. He sought to control the expansionist forces that led to the dispatch of the marines in the first place. He thus made a sustained effort to break out of the imperial Present. And that required less dependence upon open-ended expansion and more willingness to contain America itself. Trade must be redefined as the honest and useful exchange of goods and services rather than as the key to sustaining the Present.

Hoover therefore tried to persuade the Congress and other leaders to set limits, to control the possessive and mindlessly profit-oriented actions of bankers and other capitalists. He failed. But he nevertheless began to withdraw the marines from Haiti and Nicaragua and refused to send them —or even to threaten to send them—when Cubans again disturbed the American Present.

He also asked the Congress for money to help Sun Yat-sen and the Kuomintang Government of China. The legislators again refused. And then Japan attacked Manchuria. Hoover did display an understanding—a "certain" sympathy—for Japan: it needed strong economic relationships with other countries to develop its own life; China was still disorganized in the midst of revolution; and the Russians were disruptive. All very troublesome and difficult.

But Hoover did not make his decisions on the basis

of an anti-Communist crusade. He instead honored his commitment to self-determination and his sense of history. He had his priorities straight. The definition of national security is that "no foreign soldier will land on American soil." Then he laid it on the line. "To maintain forces less than that strength is to destroy national safety, to maintain greater forces is not only economic injury to our people but a threat against our neighbors and would be a righteous cause for ill will amongst them."

The Japanese attack did "not imperil the freedom of the American people, the economic future of our people. I do not propose ever to sacrifice American life for anything short of this." Then his sense of history. "No matter what Japan does in time they will not Japanify China and if they stay there long enough they will be absorbed or expelled by the Chinese." [3]

Most Americans supported that decision. But in the crunch we were not prepared to act on even Hoover's limited vision of an American Future, *not prepared to come together and function as citizens to make a new America.* Sometimes, as during the finest moments of the Great Depression, we honored our principles. People helped each other, and the more dedicated reformers struggled to devise and enact programs that would enable all of us to see ourselves as part of a community. And to act that way.

But we did not exercise the imagination and muster the courage that is required to leave the Present for the Future. And so we dug our souls—as well as our fingernails—into the crumbling sands of the Present. We had not learned from John Quincy Adams, and we did not learn from Randolph Bourne or Herbert Hoover.

[3] I am unable to refrain from pointing out how this deep perception was also a prophetic comment upon American intervention in China and Vietnam—and other places too numerous to list.

# 10
## And So Unto the Third and Fourth Crusades

You could probably fix it so that everything produced
here would be consumed here, but that would
completely change our Constitution, our very
conceptions of law. And nobody contemplates that.
Therefore, you find that you must look to other
markets and those markets are abroad. . . .
—Dean Acheson, 1944

*The United States must run this show.*
—Presidential Adviser William L. Clayton, 1947

We are willing to help people who believe the way
we do, to continue to live the way they want to live.
—Dean Acheson, 1947

Despite his inability to transcend it, the massive
breakdown of American capitalism that began in 1929 provided a traumatic footnote for Hoover's central point: the
Present would inevitably become the Past unless Americans
imagined and created a Future. Ignoring his insight, Hoover's
successors ultimately defined the Future as the Past and

embarked upon another crusade to preserve the Present. That process began, however, as a less emotional effort to maintain America's Open Door System in the face of a concerted campaign to revive the past in modern form.

# I

Fascism has often been interpreted as a conservative response to the Bolshevik Revolution in Russia and to the more general revival of socialism that followed upon that dramatic unheaval. That is a seriously incomplete analysis, and even its limited usefulness is often lost in the subsequent distortion that equated the two phenomena. Fascism began long before the rise of Adolph Hitler as an honest effort by Catholic intellectuals to draw upon the doctrines of the Church and the practices (real and imagined) of feudal society in order to create a socially responsible ideology and program for industrial society.[1] It thus rested upon the cornerstone of hierarchy: a benevolent ordering and direction of all the corporate elements of society. The truth would ultimately be implemented by all members of society as they came to recognize and honor it, but in the meantime it would be administered by the wise and knowing elders of the Church.

Socialism offered a strikingly different relationship with the Past. Marx recognized that feudalism, and even the early Church, had provided a certain kind of cooperative society; and likewise understood that the destruction of that limited community by capitalism led some people to advocate reviving that society as an alternative to the possessive individualism of the marketplace. But he considered that

[1] One group of those people soon asserted the futility of embracing the Past and instead developed a theory and program of Christian Socialism. While hardly radical, they did understand the need to move the Church into the Future.

**165**

approach to be romantic nonsense: embracing a dream and therefore settling for less than was possible. Capitalism had released vast human and natural resources that could and should now be used to create a new community of equals sharing in the making of their own Future.

Thus fascism and socialism are fundamentally different, and many Americans sensed or understood that during the late 1920s and early 1930s when Italy and Germany began to adopt and then to distort the serious ideas of fascism into a program of domestic repression and imperialism. These Americans did not like what was happening in Russia, but they did not automatically equate those events with socialism.[2] And the argument that Russia and Germany were the same did not become generally current until after 1939, when, after England and France refused to join a mutual security league with Russia, Stalin signed a non-aggression pact with Hitler.

During those same years, Americans came increasingly to feel that Japan had emulated Western economic progress without accepting the rules of international behavior that were essential to the preservation of the capitalist marketplace. The leaders in Tokyo came to be viewed as men who were not satisfied with extensive influence in China (and the rest of Asia), but seemed determined to construct an old-fashioned mercantilist empire.

The ensuing debate during the 1930s about whether those developments required the United States to go to war against Japan or Germany—or both—was blunt at the outset and became increasingly embittered. But there was not much rhetoric about another American crusade until the later stages; most of the early talk was about the necessity—or the

[2] And, for that matter, there was an upsurge of sympathy for the Soviet Union and a rise in militant radicalism in America, as the Depression became increasingly severe.

lack of it—of resorting to war to preserve the existing system. And Americans remained seriously divided about direct military intervention on the night before the Japanese bombed Pearl Harbor.

Even those who became the most militant interventionists initially laid heavy emphasis upon the practical necessity of stopping Germany and Japan. It is easy to forget—or overlook—that theme because their later arguments emphasized the need to save Civilization and Freedom. But there was much talk about markets and raw materials and the control of the seas that was considered essential to both of those elements of the Present.[3] American leaders were deeply concerned about German economic penetration in Latin America, for example, and unequivocally drew the line in Asia when Japan moved to control the resources of the rich Southeast Asian peninsula.

But American leaders also became increasingly willing to use war as a means of *extending* (rather than merely protecting) the Open Door System. They wanted to penetrate the economic empires presided over by England and France and insure American domination in other areas, as well as to free Europe from Hitler's bloody fist. That was the thrust. But, as in the years when the Open Door Policy was first formulated, the concern for economic expansion again became intermixed with a demand to extend American civilization. And civilization was individualism. No individualism, no business; and no business, no American civilization.

## II

The interventionists first appealed to the principle of self-determination in opposing Japan's expansion. That was

[3] Begin here with Lloyd Gardner, *Economic Aspects of New Deal Diplomacy* (Madison, Wisc., U. of Wisconsin Press, 1964).

natural in view of the old tie between China and the Open
Door Policy and necessary because France and England did
not move seriously toward a confrontation with Germany
until after Hitler casually violated the Munich Compromise
of 1938 by absorbing Czechoslovakia. Then the interventionists began to play all imaginable variations upon the
Wilsonian theme of saving the world for the American
Present.

The former President was discovered to have been
correct about the necessities of collective security, and the
essentials of his old program were shortly reiterated. Franklin Roosevelt first enunciated (on January 6, 1941) the Four
Freedoms (*of* speech and worship, and *from* want and fear).
It was a remarkably skillful performance based on mixing
elements from the Bill of Rights with the old conception of
a Christian American civilization, and then blending in an
appeal based on the fears (and experiences) of the Depression.

Roosevelt and British Prime Minister Winston
Spencer Churchill next issued the Atlantic Charter on August
14, 1941, a document that restated the essentials of Wilson's
Fourteen Points. The United States was not then officially
at war, but its leaders were committed to it and the navy
was already helping to destroy German submarines in the
Atlantic Ocean. By that time, most Americans undoubtedly
expected some kind of war, but they did not accept that fate
until the Japanese attack.

The confrontation with the Axis Powers that had
begun as a rather straightforward conflict of imperial systems
became a crusade undertaken to force the enemy into uncon-
ditional surrender. That, too, was a strong echo of Wilson's
determination in 1918 to apply force to Germany until it
agreed to establish a government "that we can trust." And,

168

in the narrow military sense, as with Lincoln and Wilson, Roosevelt carried his crusade to a victorious conclusion.

But once again the broad purpose of the struggle was an illusion.[4] Having failed to comprehend that the Present cannot be preserved, and failing therefore to develop a conception of the Future, they had no use for victory except as a means to sustain the Open Door System. Perhaps no leader illustrates the point better than Dean G. Acheson, a man of unusual ability who wrote poetry to his daughter about saving the world, and who joyfully exercised great influence in launching still another crusade.[5]

Acheson *prided* himself: on being a good and proper Yale Man who disdained the familiarity affected by Franklin Roosevelt (of Harvard); on being a Wilsonian who was tougher than his mentor; on spurning the feeling of regret as "that most enfeebling of emotions"; and as a gentleman who carried the Jeffersonian torch—"the hope of the world lies in the United States." Acheson's sense of noblesse oblige was broad enough to include Harry S. Truman, a tough middle-class politician from Missouri, who was a fellow Wilsonian (those "noble policies"). As President, Truman also never wasted his time on regrets: prided *himself* on never having had a second thought about using two nuclear weapons that killed hundreds of thousands of Japanese civilians.

Truman and Acheson made an awesome and effective combination, but even so they were only the tip of the iceberg known as the Cold War. Henry Luce, the Lord of the feudal barony known as *Time,* Incorporated, who con

---

[4] Here see Lloyd Gardner's subsequent book, *Architects of Illusion. Men and Ideas in American Foreign Policy, 1941–1949* (New York, Franklin Watts, 1970).

[5] See, as a beginning, the rhyme he wrote to his daughter upon the occasion of his reentry into the State Department: Acheson, *Present at the Creation* (New York, W. W. Norton, 1969), p. 121.

trolled more words than anyone else outside the government, offered and agitated his own version of The American Century. Hanson Baldwin, the esteemed realistic columnist of *The New York Times,* echoed Jefferson and Lincoln. America, "far more than any single factor, is the key to the destiny of tomorrow; we alone may be able to avert the decline of Western civilization, and a revision to nihilism and the Dark Ages." A less famous but nevertheless influential leader stuck to the traditional rhetoric: "Free enterprise cannot be confined within even our wide borders and continue to exist." And another remarked candidly that all of them were looking for "a substitute for empire."

Will Clayton, the modern master of the American cotton industry, combined the past and the present. He recalled Lincoln's dictum about America being unable to continue half-free and half-slave and applied it to postwar capitalism: if it could not expand, then it would collapse in America. The death of capitalism would mean socialism, the dreaded Future, and hence the Open Door Policy must be applied throughout the world. All action, including any that involved emergency assistance and aid for rehabilitation, must be guided by one rule: *"The United States must run this show."*

That attitude (and succinctness) not only impressed Acheson, but reinforced Truman's view. The President and Acheson shared an intense interest in the apocalyptic. The Present was threatening to come apart at the seams, and America was the only reliable tailor. Acheson told the Congress in 1944 that any effort to deal with the crisis by making structural changes would lead to the end of liberty, freedom, capitalism, and all other good things in the United States.[6] And he shared with Truman a propensity to view

[6] But again, the tip of the iceberg, for no significant group of leaders challenged him on the point.

America as another Athens or Rome girding itself to resist the onslaught of Eastern barbarians. Or as Christendom rallying the faithful against Islam.[7]

Those analogies, which revealed a brilliant ignorance and miscomprehension of history, enabled Truman, Acheson, and other American leaders once again to evade the Future. They were, indeed, the first masters of the art of the false syllogism that later came to be known as McCarthyism. Their magic worked this way: define the Future as socialism, then define socialism as what existed in Russia (and later China, etc.), and on that basis equate socialism with barbarism (and Nazi Germany). The Future thus became "reactionary in the extreme," as Acheson phrased it, and hence America was once again the noble knight of the marketplace preserving the Good Present against the Bad Past.[8]

# III

And so onward once again to counterrevolution in the name of self-determination. The American purpose, explained Acheson, "was to safeguard the highest interest of our nation, which was to maintain as spacious an environment as possible in which free states might exist and flourish." Free states were those which accepted the American Present. In Acheson's words: *"We are willing to help*

---

[7] As should by now be apparent, my use of the term *crusade* is grounded in the attitude, outlook, and language of the protagonists. I leave to other scholars any comparison with the classical crusades.

[8] Here see L. K. Adler and T. G. Paterson, "Red Fascism: The Merger of Nazi Germany and Soviet Russia in the American Image of Totalitarianism, 1930–1950s," *American Historical Review*, Vol. 75 (1970), pp. 1046–1064. McCarthy did no more than embellish and apply this false syllogism with an ambitious ruthlessness. Then see Robert Bellah, "Roots of the American Taboo," *Nation*, Vol. 219 (December 28, 1974): his perception into how the American Socialist movement after Debs suffered from a failure to understand the tie between America's historical conception of itself as Israelites or as Christian crusaders (or both) is both brilliant and crucial.

*people who believe the way we do, to continue to live the way they want to live."* Anyone who offered an alternative, or tried to implement it, was by definition misguided and dangerous.

Appropriately enough, it all began in China. Acheson candidly explained in later years that America gave much aid and comfort to Chiang Kai-shek at the end of World War II in an effort to help him establish his superiority over Mao Tse-tung while at the same time trying to persuade Mao to accept that arrangement. He admitted that the attempt failed, but then wept woefully that no other alternative offered any better prospect.

Acheson (and most others) simply could not imagine the obvious alternative: honor the principle of self-determination. Let the Chinese settle their own affairs in their own way, and then deal with the result. He saw the Future as Russia, which he had redefined as the Past, and hence the Chinese Revolution was no more than the long arm of the Past reaching once again into the Present. All part of the same conspiracy against American Christian civilization. He would deal only with the Chinese who in his estimation qualified as Chinese. Those who had become Russians were beyond the pale.

People who believe they possess The Truth do not make decisions so much as they perform the same ritual in different circumstances. So it was with Truman and Acheson, and their successors. But to fully understand them, it is necessary to make a crucial distinction about the way they acted upon their faith. They were *initially* counterrevolutionary without being wholly reactionary. They accepted and encouraged change—even fomented it—*if it sustained or enlarged America's empire for the freedom of possessive individualism.* During the early years of their reign, there-

172

fore, they can justly be compared with the great Popes and Cardinals of antiquity, who displayed flexibility and a sense of limits in the cause of the Living Church.

And, within that framework, and for a time, they often spoke candidly, and some of their works produced good consequences. Everyone involved in the Bretton Woods Monetary Conference of 1944, for example, knew that the United States was determined to establish itself as the economic center of the world and admitted that the effort had some relevance to the circumstances of the time. And all British leaders realized that the real price of the $3.5 billion loan they obtained from America in 1945 involved the penetration of their empire and the setting of severe limits on any effort to create a democratic socialism. But there was no sham on the part of American spokesmen, and the main body of British Socialists were not at all sure about how far into the Future *they* wanted to go.[9]

Truman's famous speech about aid to Greece and Turkey left no doubt that America was moving into a conception of itself as the Christian, civilizing *policeman* of the world, or that revolutions would be judged by American standards. Acheson's subsequent lecture in Mississippi spoke openly about the need to help Western Europe in order to save the Present in America, and the Marshall Plan *did* save or improve the lives of many people.

The United States also encouraged and recognized the principle of self-determination in India and Israel. The Indian story reminds one of Seward and Maximilian in Mexico. Roosevelt told Churchill that it was time to leave India, figuratively poking a finger into the Prime Minister's belly to emphasize the point. But it was the Indians, led

[9] Here see Thomas Balogh, "Keynes and the IMF," London *Times Literary Supplement* (October 10, 1975), pp. 1211–1214.

by Gandhi, who drove the real fist into the guts of that empire; and it was the quasi-Socialist Labour Government of Britain (that so troubled the sleep of Acheson, Clayton, and others) which honored the principle of self-determination. Americans had a very small part in that play.

They did star, however, as the main supporting actor in the drama of Israel. Jews initially suffered much pain and sorrow in America (and still do), but they survived and established themselves as a powerful voice among those who made the crucial decisions. Such American Jews paid for many of the machine guns and bombs that blasted Palestine out of the European imperial system and created the state of Israel. And even Americans who were anti-Semitic at home were stirred by the performance. Others felt the pull of the old American sense of mission—Israel was another City on the Hill. The United States was finally beginning, as John Winthrop and Joseph Warren had prophesied, to preserve the virtue of the world.

Hence, while Truman was undoubtedly influenced by the Jewish clout within the Democratic party, he was also beholden to Wilson's conception of self-determination. There was, indeed, no conflict of interest. The Jews, being good Americans, even one of the early images Americans had used to make sense of themselves, deserved the support of all good Americans.

But it was not that simple, for there were millions of other people in the Middle East (beginning with the Palestinians) who had an equal claim to self-determination. And Israel compounded the problem by echoing Lincoln: saying to the Palestinians, as Honest Abe had said to the southerners, that you are perfectly free to self-determine yourselves into an increasingly irrelevant minority within our Present. And American leaders said Amen.

## IV

That was the beginning of the end of what little remained of the American commitment to the principle of self-determination. That process involved interlocking ironies that can be viewed as the ultimate expression of the contradiction inherent in trying to preserve the Present. Secretary of the Navy James V. Forrestal argued strongly against neglecting the Arab right to self-determination within the Open Door System—after all, they had the oil. But at the same time, he became the most influential patron of a bright and ambitious foreign service officer named George Frost Kennan, who argued that it was essential to confront Russian totalitarianism with unanswerable force on every front because expansionism was the touchstone of the Soviet system.

Kennan was a bureaucratic spokesman of the doctrine espoused by Madison and Jefferson, Congressman Delano and Lincoln, and intellectuals like Frederick Jackson Turner, Brooks Adams, and Woodrow Wilson—to say nothing of Acheson of Yale. Kennan did not know enough history to realize that he was one of them, that his argument was but another version of their argument: if expansion is necessary to the American way, then containment is death. Lincoln followed that logic in developing his doctrine of containing slavery. Adams used the verb "to contain" in 1900 when he proposed a similar policy toward Russia. All Kennan did was to carry the holy doctrine into the 1940s.

Then matters became even more complicated. Forrestal embraced Kennan's argument. But so did Acheson and Truman. The only trouble was that they read it to mean that Israel was the bastion of strength to prevent the

**175**

Soviets from controlling the Middle East by appealing to and helping the Arabs. That, very simply, meant that Israel became the potential Fort Sumter of the twentieth century.

Acheson viewed Kennan's analysis as a useful footnote to support his own thesis. It *was* true that Kennan's metaphors were more than a bit bourgeois: he talked in middle-class terms about the Soviets as a windup toy that could only be stopped by an American wall. Even so, he also revealed a propensity to speak of deeper matters like Civilization. Acheson put it very neatly when he defined the American Present as being "the only kind of world" in which civilization *could* exist.

Thus Acheson used Kennan against other equally intelligent and thoughtful bureaucrats within the State Department. And to fight all others who suggested that it might be useful—even vital—"to reexamine all our policies and all our programs." Acheson gives the game away: there was a very tough argument within the State Department (and with some elements in the Congress) about whether it was historically accurate—*and therefore wise, let alone practical*—to accept the Kennan analysis of Soviet behavior. The doubters advanced impressive arguments that Stalin (and others) sought first and primarily the security to self-determine their own revolution.[10]

Acheson the Yale Man knew The Truth, and so had no patience with such serious and consequential dialogue. He was saving civilization and the individualistic marketplace—the American Christian Present. He considered the debate "a stultifying and, so I thought, sterile argument." And he had the power to pick the winners. Thus the final

[10] Gardner explores the Forrestal-Kennan relationship in *Architects of Illusion*. Acheson reveals the guts of the story in *Present at the Creation*. For an example of the dissent, see G. A. Morgan, "Stalin on Revolution," *Foreign Affairs*, Vol. 27 (1949); and M. D. Shulman, *Stalin's Foreign Policy Reappraised* (Cambridge, Harvard U. Press, 1963).

irony. He chose Kennan's argument even as Kennan began to look for a way to escape the consequences of his inflexible metaphors.

That decision led to a long and elaborate statement of the thinking behind the newest crusade: an American Papal Bull. Known formally as National Security Council Document 68 (NSC-68), it ostensibly remained TOP SECRET for many years; but, as Acheson has admitted, he talked about it so often, and so much of it was leaked to various sympathetic observers, that there was never any mystery about its main themes.[11]

First: the success of the Russian Revolution threatens the American Present.

Second: to preserve that Present, "the nation must be determined, at whatever cost or sacrifice, to preserve at home and abroad those conditions of life."

Third: "this means virtual abandonment by the United States of trying to distinguish between national and global security. . . . Security must henceforth become the dominant element in the national budget, and other elements must be accommodated to it."

That outlook led inevitably to war: first in Korea, and then elsewhere. An argument of sorts can be made, of course, for insisting that the South Koreans should be allowed to remain within the Open Door System until they began their own revolution. That is probably the best case that can be offered in behalf of empire. But the crucial point is that Acheson and Truman had no hesitation in using force to dishonor even that imperial ideal.

They were, like Lincoln and Wilson, determined to grab hold of history and make it conform to the American

---

[11] The document was declassified in April, 1975. The formal title is "United States Objectives and Programs for National Security, 14 April 1950."

Present.[12] They undertook to *self-determine* all of Korea as an element of the Open Door Present. They did it knowing that the Chinese would intervene. And so they were the worst McCarthyites of all: they used General Douglas MacArthur to hide the true nature of their crusade.

Acheson tells us in his memoirs that China said unequivocally on October 5, 1950, "that if American troops crossed the [38th] parallel China would enter the war." Then he arrogantly asserts that the remark was "not an authoritative statement of policy." But it was made to the Indian ambassador in China who was being used by Acheson as his source of accurate information about China.

He and Truman thought that they had the power and so sent the General north. He was clobbered. Which meant that many of his soldiers were killed. So MacArthur was fired, and the lesson was not learned. Not by MacArthur, who kept insisting that a few atomic bombs would preserve the American Present forever; not by Truman and Acheson; and not by their successors, who thought they possessed magic unknown to their predecessors.

We all know the rest of the story. It is not a pleasant tale, and my citizen's soul is weary under the burden of my knowledge of my country dishonoring its once noble commitment to the right of self-determination. I leave it to others to reveal the details of the sagas of the terrible and bloody deeds of the Central Intelligence Agency and the Federal Bureau of Investigation, and to retell and embellish the grisly truths about Iran and Guatemala, Indonesia and Santo Domingo, Italy and Cuba, and Vietnam and Watergate. And Chile. Perhaps most of all Chile. For

---

[12] Here I am paraphrasing the basic conclusion of Gaddis Smith in his study of Acheson's attitude: "Only the United States had the power to grab hold of history and make it conform." Gaddis Smith in *Dean Acheson*, ed. by Robert H. Ferrel (New York, Cooper Square Publishers, 1972), p. 416.

there we purposely destroyed a man who was dedicated to making a peaceful transition into the Future. Jefferson trembled for his country. In deep and quiet anger, I weep for mine.

# V

So we come to the end of the Present. The evidence is too vast even to quantify with a computer. Think only of Wilson sending Debs to jail and refusing to pardon him *even after the war was won*. Then think of President Gerald Ford pardoning Richard Nixon, not just for Watergate, but for *any and all crimes* Nixon may have committed. The more things stay the same the more they stay the same.

But the most revealing evidence lies in the decline of American conservatism. America has always been conservative, hence that is the telltale record of the heartbeat of our health as a society and a culture. And Hoover was the last great conservative. He warned Truman to relax: "our position should be to persuade . . . [to] hold up the banner of free peoples and let it go at that for the present." He was ignored. Then he said America should come home to the Western Hemisphere and get on with imagining and creating its own Future. And for that he was called "a tool of the Kremlin." The last act of McCarthyism—written and performed by an all-star stable of liberals, radicals, and reactionaries.

Oh yes, there were Robert Taft and Walter Lippmann, but neither of them had a vision of an American Future. Taft thought conservatism meant preserving, and Lippmann thought it was surviving. Neither is true conservatism. As Randolph Bourne cried out in anguish about Dewey, it is all a pot of pragmatism.

And so we are left with Hoover. He was not as towering a figure as the earlier giants like Jonathan Edwards and John Quincy Adams, but he understood the necessity of accepting the Future and the vital importance of honoring the bedrock principle of self-determination. And he, as well as they, knew that crusades to self-determine other people in our own image involved the fundamental denial of that ideal.

That principle lies at the center of our American tradition and, to recall the great line by William Butler Yeats, when that center is not held as life itself then life itself dribbles away into various imperial adventures.

And so unto our own day. In one sense, of course, Henry Kissinger has earned our respect: he says candidly that he is trying to preserve the Present. So honor him for his honesty and marvel at his inability to understand the futility of his crusade. He ought in truth to forget about Prince Metternich and do some homework on John Quincy Adams and Herbert Hoover.

And the rest of us should begin the long and arduous work of self-determining our Future as Americans.

# Conclusion
# Let Us Make
# Our Own Future
# with the Help of the Past

We are all inextricably locked into the past, and the choice is between imprisoning oneself in the past and taking rational, innovatory steps into the future.
—Historian Moses I. Finley, 1975

You must abolish the system or accept its consequences.
—Orestes Brownson, 1840

He who desires but acts not, breeds pestilence.
—William Blake, *The Marriage of Heaven and Hell*

Thou wilt find rest from vain fancies if thou doest every act in life as though it were thy last.
—Marcus Aurelius Antoninus, *Meditations*, II, 5

We have been playing hide-and-seek for two centuries on the basis of a gentleman's agreement never to run off into either the Past or the Future. That has nevertheless left us with a large playground, perhaps best epitomized in this motto: "Limbo Is Our Way of Life."

Prospering in limbo *is* an unusual achievement. Perhaps, as Bismarck commented, we have enjoyed a special dispensation from God. Those inclined to that explanation would do well to remember, however, that the German Prince linked us with fools as being the two particular concerns of the Lord. And also to recall Jefferson's somber remark about trembling for us because he knew that God was just. On the other hand, we may owe it all to nothing more mysterious than vast resources, fortuitous circumstances, and superior firepower.

Explain it as you will, America has until recently defied Time. We have been so effective in preserving the Present, however, that we have failed to realize that it is rapidly becoming archaic. Even more disturbing, we have hardly noticed that we have paid in the coin of our heritage. We have forgotten what it is to self-determine ourselves.

It may well be too late. I do not say that with finality, but as a citizen and as a historian I have to admit the possibility. And if all that the rumors of catastrophe mean (à la Acheson) is that the barbarians will land at Plymouth Rock, I can only say that I will give over in peace. They would move us off dead center. But I see no true barbarians on the horizon: certainly not the Russians. Everyone with the interest in conquering us, or the power to do so, is lusting for our Present. A dreary prospect.

Which confronts us with the challenge of being our own barbarians. Viewed superficially, as bombs assembled in the basement and then secreted in toilets on the thirtieth floor, or as shooting Presidents and other factotums, that is not a meaningful choice. That is silly self-indulgence. But taken seriously, as an effort to create for the first time an American Future, it is an exciting challenge. To be a contemporary barbarian is to use our revolutionary right of self-determination to create a community in place of a marketplace; to replace the impersonal logic of possessive

182

individualism with the morality of helping each of us cherish the other.

# I

Let us begin by saying simply that James Madison was a highly intelligent person who was as wrong as anyone can be. He argued that expansion underwrites freedom, but the truth is that expansion is nothing more than a polite word for empire. And empire is the end of freedom. At home as well as abroad. John Quincy Adams finally got it right: to embark upon an effort to save the world is to destroy ourselves as well as many parts of the world. Probably all of it.

Let us next admit that Lincoln (*and* Wilson *and* Acheson) were giants who fudged the central issue. Once we began to hedge the right of self-determination in the name of our Present, we began to take our rewards in the goodies of the imperial marketplace and in the false coin of self-righteousness. It is not pleasant to root out and then turn away from the deadly weaknesses and evasions of those we have trusted and honored. But so be it if it is so revealed. We have no choice but to self-determine ourselves or die.

So we must face the question of how to begin, what to seek, and how to continue the voyage. Let us first go back to Madison and turn him inside out. Instead of enlarging the sphere, let us work our way toward the goal of creating several small spheres that will be communities. The very idea of an imperial community is, upon even the most cursory examination, a contradiction in terms—a denial of the premise in the program to realize the premise. If the objective is to govern a continent under one system, then it can only be done as an empire. Consider not only

America. Look at Russia, India, and Brazil. Even China, although we can learn important things from Mao's efforts to devise a way out of the dilemma.

Hence we must move another step into the Past beyond Madison. Unlike Lincoln, we must seek to honor rather than to supersede our revolutionary forefathers. That means evoking and using the Past to create a Future that honors our primary commitment to self-determination. We must return therefore to the Articles of Confederation. That document offers us a base from which to begin our voyage into a human Future; a model of government grounded in the idea and the ideal of self-determined communities coming together as equals when and as it is necessary to combine forces to honor common values and realize common objectives.

Many years ago I argued that the Articles were unsuited to their time.[1] I would stick with the essence of that judgment: newly independent societies require a sustained and coordinated effort to survive, develop their own identities, and establish their political economies. That is the underlying explanation of the rise of mercantilism during the latter part of the sixteenth century. It also goes far to account for the distortions of socialism and communism in the twentieth century. They were conceived as postcapitalist models for an industrialized community, not as a way of transcending economic weakness and the social fragmentation generated by modernization.

But I have become steadily more impressed with the vision that produced the Articles. They represented a profound perception that the human dilemma is not defined by a simple choice between survival or honoring one's ideals. They speak to the truth that we struggle to honor our ideals. Otherwise we become the walking dead. And deadly.

[1] *The Contours of American History* (Cleveland, World Publishing Co., 1961), p. 121.

Viewed in that light, the Constitution deserves our respect as an unusually sophisticated statement of the argument that we honor our ideals only as we survive. Our respect, but neither our agreement nor our veneration. For survival at the price of institutionalizing domestic and global empire, *and internalizing empire as a way of thought and life*, is to rob our soul to feed our belly.

## II

Harsh words. I stand on them. The Constitution, to borrow a telling phrase from Jean-Paul Sartre, is a room with no exit. If you accept its essential philosophy because you want to preserve the Present, then you cannot change its essentials because that would be to risk the Present. Thus, to paraphrase Warren Susman, you endlessly redecorate the room because you dare not move to another.

The image of robbing the soul to feed the belly can also be interpreted as defining one as an idealist rather than a realist. Some might enjoy the witty thrust that I am using Christ against Marx. It is a clever but essentially irrelevant comment. Both systems, like the one created by Freud, are grand and noble metaphors describing the human condition and offering ways to realize our full potential. The central problem, however, has never been to reconcile Freud and Marx, or Christ and Marx, but rather to integrate the Marx of the Old Testament and the Marx of the New Testament.[2] For otherwise our souls are full and our bellies empty, or our bellies full and our souls empty.

[2] The issue here is the thrust of what Marx wrote before *The Communist Manifesto* (1843) as compared with what he wrote after that tour-de-force of history and incitement to revolution. I do not think that there is any serious problem in reconciling the moral Marx with Marx the analytic scholar of capitalism. But the issue has padded the bibliographies of many scholars. Here see David McLellan, *Karl Marx, His Life and Thought.* (New York, Harper and Row, 1975); and Charles Taylor, *Hegel* (Cambridge, Cambridge U. Press, 1975).

There is in the Old Testament Marx a candid recognition and acceptance of the truth that we humans cannot get enough soul food if all we concentrate on is feeding our bellies. It is as important to be free and human, and to deal with others as equal members of the community, as it is to be satiated with yummies from the store. *Any* store. The New Testament Marx never recants that truth, but he is more than a bit bedazzled by the material wonders of capitalist industrialism.

He more than occasionally sounds euphoric: we now have the power to fill *all* bellies *all* the time *and* to be free. But if one overlooks the exaggeration of exuberance one must give him his due: he just might have squared that circle. A challenging case can be made that if Western Europe and the United States had turned to socialism during the 1870s, then the world would have enjoyed an equilibrium between the soul and the belly and that the Socialist ethic would have enabled us to deal with the problem of finite resources in an equitable and humane fashion.

But that did not happen, and we are today confronted with honoring the Old Testament Marx by imagining and then creating our own New Testament. It may sound a bit disrespectful—some will no doubt say irreligious—but I think he would enjoy a bit of blunt talk. If his First Coming failed to meet its schedule (and was thereby distorted by those who tried to force it past its time), then we will have to arrange the Second Coming on our own. I think Marx would not only approve but feel betrayed if we failed to try.

### III

We must begin, each of us, with ourselves. I do not mean psychoanalysis or group therapy or transcendental meditation. Each of those is helpful for some people in some circumstances at some time. But I am talking about acting as thoughtful and militant *citizens*. That is not only excellent therapy, but it is the essence of liberation and community— of self-determination.

The true destructiveness of our concern to preserve the Present lies in the way it has limited and confined our basic sense of self-determination. It is not simply that males have defined females as housewives and sex objects. Or that whites have viewed colored people as inferior. It is equally deadly for females to accept (implicitly or otherwise) the male definition of self-determination as *macho* success in the marketplace, or for Blacks and Reds to seek fulfillment in putting the whites down on the mud sill. All that is understandable and natural, and some of it is necessary and healthy; but none of it is meaningful as a definition of citizenship in a community.

A citizen is a person who knows—and honors—the truth that he or she can fulfill himself or herself only as a member of a community. In the end, therefore, we have to say no to empire, for it is a contradiction in terms to talk about being a citizen in an empire. Some people feel that ending the war in Vietnam and driving Nixon from office created a momentum for change. But it is impossible to end the empire, either at home or abroad, by winning occasional dramatic victories. Particularly when they are in truth but marginal victories. The structural determinants of another imperial war, and for another effort to consolidate total power, remain essentially as strong as ever. A massive and centralized empire absorbs such setbacks, even calls them defeats, as a sponge absorbs water. It is all very well to argue that enough water will saturate the sponge, but that will also very probably inundate us along with the leaders of the empire.

Therein lies the problem. We can benefit from exter-

WILLIAM APPLEMAN WILLIAMS

nal pressures on the empire, or gross abuses within the empire, only if we are ready to act at home. So we are back with the importance of being citizens. If that begins, as I think it does, with a commitment to community and to the best of our heritage, rather than to the mirage of a free marketplace or the narcissistic dream of self-selected and self-sufficient cadres, then it moves next to acting as a citizen in one's own neighborhood. That means, as a start, nothing more dramatic than opening oneself to know other people. First to learn their names, and to use them at every opportunity. Then to learn their concerns, and how they think and feel about dealing with those difficulties. Finally, to understand their dreams and visions and to talk with them about how to translate them into reality.

It all sounds very elementary and time-consuming, and it *is* very elementary and time-consuming. But it has to be done if one is to be a citizen embarked upon the adventure of building a self-determined community. After that, moreover, the labor grows even more difficult. Moving out of a neighborhood in which you have earned your way as a citizen into the city or the state is a demanding experience. It is going back to being alone and in today's America made even more painful because there are so few neighborhoods sure enough of themselves to welcome a stranger as a fellow citizen. But it has to be done. Not by all of us all of the time, but by all of us some of the time. It cannot be left to the politicians simply because it ceases to be self-determination if we delegate it to someone else.

The saving grace is that each of us has our particular way of moving to and fro between our own neighborhood and the larger society. All of us have that ability. The issue is to use it. Some of us write, not just books or articles, but, even more important, letters to friends and to newspapers and magazines to discuss the issues involved in building a community. Others have different skills which open the way to becoming fellow citizens. There are those who create that feeling and reality with few if any words: they bring alive the reality of community simply by helping countless people. And there are those gifted few who publicly personify the ideal. They know and respect our concerns, our ideals, and our visions. They become leaders, and so long as they honor the community they deserve to be treasured and supported. Otherwise send them back to the neighborhood to begin again.

## IV

I have been trying, of course, to describe the process whereby you and I as individuals benumbed by the empire begin to function as citizens and then come together with countless others to create a social movement strong enough to leave the Present for a better life of our own creation. We cannot do it any other way.

It is possible, of course, to change the rulers of an empire by staging a coup. But, even if the new leaders want to alter the structure, they cannot do so *democratically* unless they represent and are supported by a social movement. If they substitute force, then they dishonor their avowed ideals and become another group of imperial overlords. Christ, for example, did not make his revolution by assassinating Pontius Pilate and installing his disciples as the top bureaucrats of the system.

Neither did Lenin, despite all the talk (including his) about the seizure of power by a minority of a minority. Lenin and the Bolsheviks took power as the vanguard of a broad social movement committed to changing the structure of Russian society. The subsequent failure to respond to the various elements in that movement—and the consequent necessity to substitute force for community—does not change the essential nature of the Revolution. Lenin acted in the name of a social movement that had been developing since 1825 and which survives today through such courageous and thoughtful people as Roy Medvedev.[3]

The central point has been made many times since the Russian Revolution. One thinks immediately of the Chinese revolutionaries led first by Sun Yat-sen and then by Mao Tse-tung. They saw themselves as expressions and agents of a vast upwelling of people who knew that a better life depended upon changing the structure of Chinese society. Mao understood the two essentials better than almost anyone. The right of self-determination is in truth an ongoing revolutionary process that must be honored into the Future. But it is not another name for anarchy, and hence we have to agree upon limits. That poses an extremely difficult problem, but then that is the definition of life.

Then one thinks of India and Cuba. India is turning toward despotism because Gandhi's successors failed to recognize the difference between a political party and a social movement. A party rules people, whereas a social movement creates a community. Castro sensed that crucial distinction and has tried—with increasing success—to use his power to create a community. The "Maximum Leader" has a vision of making himself incidental: of using his charisma to insure his ultimate irrelevance.

Hence it is important to understand the nature of a social movement. It is, to begin with, not an interest group, not even a large one, for the members of such a group are concerned primarily (if not exclusively) with their particular objectives. Nor is it a group of people who come together from different backgrounds to accomplish one specific task.

[3] *On Socialist Democracy* (New York, Alfred A. Knopf, 1975).

The project to put a man on the moon illustrates the different nature of such activities. The people in the space program shared a common interest, compromised various conflicts in order to realize one objective, and enjoyed a limited kind of camaraderie. But they were not united by a common concern with the nature and quality of life, and most of them spun off to other things when the particular job was finished.

The struggle to end the war in Vietnam involved more of the elements that define a social movement and for a short period gave promise of transcending its immediate objective. One dynamic and imaginative group of people in the coalition was unquestionably concerned with developing an alternate conception of America,[4] and it proved able for a time to work with other groups who were not initially or primarily interested in that objective. That crucial capacity to function as a citizen working with others to evolve a mutually self-determined future was aborted by a combination of impatience, elitism, the lack of any real consequential sense of history, and the failure to offer even a meaningful outline for a different America. The antiwar coalition thus became a single-issue pressure group that began to disintegrate even before the war was actually terminated—though it clearly made an important contribution to that result.

By contrast, a social movement generates its own objectives rather than coming into existence to implement or oppose decisions made by others and is deeply involved with the fundamental issues of the political economy. It may (and often does) begin in the herky-jerky dissatisfactions of unassociated people about their existing circumstances and

---

[4] While the Students for a Democratic Society are usually noted at this point, it is important to realize that *there were many other students and nonacademics* who were initially excited by and involved in the exploration of specific and vague alternatives to the existing imperial system.

**191**

their anger toward those they hold responsible for their unhappy predicament. But to become a social movement, those people must agree to compromise their different immediate interests and lifestyles *in order to create a different way of life.*

Hence we must develop a vision. The term *vision* sounds romantic, even mystical, but it is essentially practical. The Monroe Doctrine and the Open Door Policy, for example, were visions, but they were also very earthy conceptions of how to organize the world. A vision is an ordering of values in an ideal way. An organization of reality as we would like it to be. Hence it is a religious experience. Once again, as when in the introduction I defined *structural,* I go to the dictionary: religion involves a "code of ethics." To be religious, therefore, means to acknowledge, and to do one's very best to honor in practice, a system of values. Such a structure of ideals may or may not invoke the name of God in the biblical sense, but it must provide *some* injunction to do certain things and not to do other things.

It all means, and sooner rather than later, that we who want to move beyond the Present must commit ourselves to a new ethical system. The private gain and private pleasure of possessive individualism must give way to helping other people. Must give way, that is, to being citizens of a community.[5]

Such an alternate conception of life involves three major elements. First, a combination of new values and a revised ranking of the old values that are considered important to honor. Second, new institutions and rules (and modifications of the old ones) designed to implement the new hierarchy of values. Third, a continuing willingness to tolerate and compromise secondary differences in order to translate the vision into reality—into a community.

[5] Joseph P. Lyford, "Breakdown of Community," *The Center Magazine* (November-December, 1975), pp. 38–51.

Creating a social movement in contemporary America poses an extremely difficult challenge even if we assume that a significant number of people begin to act as citizens in their neighborhoods and the immediately larger units of the existing empire. Once people stop saying, "Oh, hell, *I* can't do anything," because they have discovered that they *can* affect and change their existing life and environment, they soon begin to ask, "What can we do about the *real* causes of our troubles?" I do not think that there is any consequential answer—theoretical or practical—to that question within the existing system.

We have been reforming America since it was consolidated as a Constitutional empire, and we have ended in an imperial mess. Our rulers are unable to disengage from even the most obvious mistakes in foreign policy with any intelligence and morality, or grace and dignity, and they continue to pout and whine about (and intervene in the affairs of) most of the people with whom we share the globe. They do not offer their ostensible fellow citizens at home any meaningful work despite a list of vast and pressing needs that requires countless books to enumerate. And what we call our social fabric is so sundered by conflicts of color, sex, and class that much of the time it reminds one of the emperor's new clothes. It is fair enough to blame *Them*, but the truth of it is that *We* continue to allow a tiny minority to control our political economy (and hence our lives) as their private pastime. The system survives through inertia and even more because no vital alternative has been proposed and agitated.

# V

So once again let us return to the Articles of Confederation. I suggest that we embark upon a sustained effort to organize a social movement dedicated to replacing the

American empire with a federation of regional communities. No euphemisms and no talk about reform. The objective is to create a federation of democratic Socialist communities.

The politics of that proposal are difficult for two reasons. It is impossible to begin by organizing a continental social movement. At the same time, we all know that the boundaries of the states have almost no ultimate relevance to the basic problems that have to be dealt with in order to change the existing structure and create a more humane society. Even so, I see no other place to initiate a radical strategy. Thus I suggest that we learn something from the Old South about how to practice the theory of self-determination.

Each of our contemporary states does retain a significant sense of identity despite a century of domestic imperialism that has centralized and consolidated power in Washington in the name of efficiency, reform, and mission. I have experienced that self-consciousness in Iowa, Texas, Wisconsin, and Oregon and have observed it in many other states. That spirit, and the related anger about further encroachments upon self-determination, can be encouraged in the name of democratic Socialist communities just as Georgia and South Carolina built upon it to create a movement for southern independence.

Radicals seem forever unable to understand that states' rights can be invoked and honored to create a Socialist community as well as to defend slavery (or other conservative and reactionary objectives).[6] That provides a sad but nevertheless revealing example of America's general lack of a true sense of history. But there is no reason, for example,

[6] For example: petroleum and its related products (such as gas) are a *social* resource. So, also, are railroads. Hence such means to our human welfare should be managed by people elected by those who define the need.

why the citizens of any state whose political economy is dominated by a few corporations cannot muster their will and transform the monsters into instruments of community welfare. Orestes Brownson had it right: "You must abolish the system or accept its consequences." The point is to stop wasting one's time trying to housebreak a beast that inevitably conditions or intimidates its ostensible trainers.

Two political strategies can be pursued simultaneously, much as Sam Adams and others did during the decade prior to the Revolution of 1776. There is no rational argument against using the existing electoral system *if* it is done openly in the name of a federation of democratic Socialist communities and *if* it is undertaken, not with a desire to be defeated, but with a desire to attract non-Socialist support on the basis of a positive vision of the future.

But it is also essential to create alternate institutions that maintain constant pressure on the imperial bureaucracies. It matters far less what they are called than that they do the homework and display the will required to force the system on the defensive. None of us likes to be nagged, particularly by people who have their facts straight and who keep on coming, and for that reason such nagging is an effective tactic in a prerevolutionary situation. Consider, as an illustration, the achievement of a group of students at Oregon State University (considered by most radicals as well as most conservatives to be a cow college that will still be there after all the others have jumped over the moon). Initially concerned only with ecological issues, they gradually became an extralegal standing Ways and Means Committee concerned with all primary issues affecting the people in the state. They are inspiring in their effectiveness and perhaps even more so because of their total lack of fear for the future.

Such groups will continue to be essential in the Future. Just as it is impossible to create a democratic socialist com-

195

munity without tough and committed citizen involvement, so will it be impossible to sustain that better life without the same kind of determination to maintain the reality of self-determination. The price of liberty is not so much vigilance as it is involvement. If you want to rest, vote for a dictator.

## VI

The crucial arena for such citizen groups is and will remain the states. That is where social movements have to be built, and they are the units for building coalitions to deal with regional and federal issues. Some existing boundaries will need to be modified as we create regional commonwealths, and the largest cities should become regions in their own right, but even then the subdivisions that we think of as states will remain essential to democratic socialism.

In the meantime, moreover, social movements within the states can accomplish far more than has generally been attempted since the heyday of Georgia, South Carolina, and Mississippi. The environmental laws and programs in California and Oregon illustrate the practicality of that logic, as does the recently enacted election law in Texas that requires those who make illegal campaign contributions to compensate the opponent over whom they sought criminal advantage.

The vitality and power of such community politics provide the only way to prevent regions from becoming bureaucratic morasses and to insure that the decisions of those dealing with federal matters will not be abstract and elitist. The decentralization of the existing American empire does not provide a guarantee of democratic equity, it only offers a human scale for action and government within which a social movement can operate effectively to create that kind of community. With that ever in mind, let us explore the outlines of one such region—a Pacific Northwest Community—that is eminently feasible.

We begin with the states of Washington, Oregon, Idaho, and Montana. Assume that we have created in each of those states a social movement that is capable of dealing with many problems and exploring many opportunities within those limits. Which is to say that we are willing and able to confront the power of corporations, the issue of priorities for the use of resources, the question of our relationship with other regions in the world, and have evolved a hierarchy of values to guide us in our life together. And, because names are important, let us, in honor of the Americans who first lived here, call our region *Neahkahnie* (Nee-ah-*kahn*-ie).

We citizens of those states are now aware, and will know even more intimately at that point, that the lives of all of us in the Pacific Northwest are irrevocably intertwined and mutually dependent upon each other. We do have common problems and share a way of life, and those provide us with the basis for developing a vision of a meaningful future. As part of that awareness, we know that some of us, particularly in Oregon and Montana, have potentially more affinity with other regions.

Parts of Oregon have a natural association with a community that reaches into California and Nevada, and perhaps even into other existing states. In a similar way, Idaho and Montana will probably divide: some sections will join us while others will find a more congenial affiliation east of the Rockies. Nor can we gloss over the need for *Neahkahnie* to evolve a close relationship with British Columbia. Therein lies a dynamic element in realizing Marx's vision of international solidarity. Once we begin to end the empire in America, we will exert pressure for similar reorganizations throughout the world. People working out their relationships with a new America will be influenced not only by our example, but by the practical necessity of acting in different ways.

That will also be true of the regional communities within America. The new federalism will be based on three kinds of fundamental agreement. The first concerns a firm commitment to basic rights as a condition of membership in the federation. We can begin with the Bill of Rights and move on through other political, and social and economic, foundations of a democratic socialist community. The second involves procedures for reaching and implementing federal decisions. The third is defined by the ongoing negotiations between such regional communities as they deal with routine economic relationships. Each of us can and must offer suggestions in each area, but that can become meaningful only as we begin to create a social movement dedicated to the basic objective.

Even as we gather strength, we will face three kinds of criticism which will often be offered by the same people. The first is that socialism inevitably means less rather than more self-determination. I can reply only that yes, it will mean less self-determination for those who now exercise monopoly power over most aspects of life for the rest of us. But the kind of socialism that I am advocating is based upon the replacement of the existing empire by regional communities of a human scale governed through democratic procedures. We will require plans, but we now live (if that is the word) under plans devised by a tiny elite: I am proposing plans suited to our respective conceptions of community. Finally, I do not advocate the total nationalization of the economy. Once we set our goals and establish our priorities, I think we should rely heavily on cooperative action to realize our objectives.

Second, we will be attacked for advocating or condoning violence. Here again I can only respond by saying, yes, there will be some violence. But not mindless or irrelevant violence. There is a vital difference between advocating violence and reluctantly accepting violence. When one is concerned, as I am, to build a social movement to change the structure of one's own society, one does not advocate violence. One seeks instead to persuade one's fellow citizens to participate in the enterprise, to join in the adventure, to walk arm in arm into the Future. To murder a President is to give up, admit defeat, surrender, commit suicide. And to murder fellow citizens with bombs placed in random toilets in random banks is to file a petition of moral, political, and intellectual bankruptcy.

But inevitably there will be some violence. How much will depend upon how many people remain actively opposed to the ideal of a self-determined community. If you are determined to prevent the creation of that kind of life, or if you think that you have the answer for all the rest of us and are determined to impose it upon us, then so be it: I will meet you on the barricades.

Third, we will be told (as even orthodox reformers are told) that our revolution will weaken America's power in the world. Again, I answer yes. If you judge power only by contemporary imperial criteria, then America will become weaker. Indeed, that is implicit in the proposal for a social movement to create the new federation. Such an America will not try to police the world, or even any part of it, and it will not attempt to expand the area of freedom by subverting the self-determination of other peoples.

But I am not saying, as so many critics charge, that a new America will be isolationist or indifferent to its security. As suggested by the example of a Pacific Northwest Community developing a close relationship with British Columbia, such an America will evolve alternate and more equitable associations with other societies. And such a new America will have considerable power and influence of a different and more consequential kind than that displayed by the existing imperial system.

That does not mean it will be eternally safe. Anyone who tells you that about any society is either a fool or a knave. Hence all I can say to you is that I prefer to die as a free man struggling to create a human community than as a pawn of empire.

So make *your* choice. Continue the treadmill exercise of trying to preserve the Present, or accept the challenge of creating our own Future. But at least make it as the decision of a consciously self-determined human being who understands what is involved and is ready to accept the consequences.

Let us together find rest from vain fancies.

# Appendix

# The Articles of Confederation
# and Perpetual Union

BETWEEN THE STATES OF NEW HAMPSHIRE, MASSACHUSETTS
BAY, RHODE ISLAND AND PROVIDENCE PLANTATIONS, CONNEC-
TICUT, NEW YORK, NEW JERSEY, PENNSYLVANIA, DELAWARE,
MARYLAND, VIRGINIA, NORTH CAROLINA, SOUTH CAROLINA,
GEORGIA.[1]

ARTICLE 1. The stile of this confederacy shall be "The
United States of America."

ART. 2. Each State retains its sovereignty, freedom and independence, and every power, jurisdiction, and right, which is
not by this confederation expressly delegated to the United
States, in Congress assembled.

ART. 3. The said states hereby severally enter into a firm
league of friendship with each other for their common defence, the security of their liberties and their mutual and
general welfare; binding themselves to assist each other
against all force offered to, or attacks made upon them, or

[1] From the *Journals,* 9:907–925, November 15, 1777.

any of them, on account of religion, sovereignty, trade, or any other pretence whatever.

ART. 4. The better to secure and perpetuate mutual friendship and intercourse among the people of the different states in this union, the free inhabitants of each of these states, paupers, vagabonds, and fugitives from justice excepted, shall be entitled to all privileges and immunities of free citizens in the several states; and the people of each State shall have free ingress and regress to and from any other State, and shall enjoy therein all the privileges of trade and commerce, subject to the same duties, impositions, and restrictions, as the inhabitants thereof respectively; provided, that such restrictions shall not extend so far as to prevent the removal of property, imported into any State, to any other State of which the owner is an inhabitant; provided also, that no imposition, duties, or restriction, shall be laid by any State on the property of the United States, or either of them.

If any person guilty of, or charged with treason, felony, or other high misdemeanor in any State, shall flee from justice and be found in any of the United States, he shall, upon demand of the governor or executive power of the State from which he fled, be delivered up and removed to the State having jurisdiction of his offence.

Full faith and credit shall be given in each of these states to the records, acts, and judicial proceedings of the courts and magistrates of every other State.

ART. 5. For the more convenient management of the general interests of the United States, delegates shall be annually appointed, in such manner as the legislature of each State shall direct, to meet in Congress, on the 1st Monday in November in every year, with a power reserved to each State to recall its delegates, or any of them, at any time within the year, and to send others in their stead for the remainder of the year.

No State shall be represented in Congress by less than two, nor more than seven members; and no person shall be capable of being a delegate for more than three years in any term of six years; nor shall any person, being a delegate, be capable of holding any office under the United States, for which he, or any other for his benefit, receives any salary, fees, or emolument of any kind.

Each State shall maintain its own delegates in a meeting of the states, and while they act as members of the committee of the states.

In determining questions in the United States, in Congress assembled, each State shall have one vote.

Freedom of speech and debate in Congress shall not be impeached or questioned in any court or place out of Congress: and the members of Congress shall be protected in their persons from arrests and imprisonments, during the time of their going to and from, and attendance on Congress, *except for treason*, felony, or breach of the peace.

ART. 6. No State, without the consent of the United States, in Congress assembled, shall send any embassy to, or receive any embassy from, or enter into any conference, agreement, alliance, or treaty with any king, prince, or state; nor shall any person, holding any office of profit or trust under the United States, or any of them, accept of any present, emolument, office or title, of any kind whatever, from any king, prince, or foreign state; nor shall the United States, in Congress assembled, or any of them, grant any title of nobility.

No two or more states shall enter into any treaty, confederation, or alliance, whatever, between them, without the consent of the United States, in Congress assembled, specifying accurately the purposes for which the same is to be entered into, and how long it shall continue.

No State shall lay any imposts or duties which may interfere with any stipulations in treaties entered into by the United States, in Congress assembled, with any king, prince, or state, in pursuance of any treaties already proposed by Congress to the courts of France and Spain.

No vessels of war shall be kept up in time of peace by any State, except such number only as shall be deemed necessary by the United States, in Congress assembled, for the defence of such State or its trade, nor shall any body of forces be kept up by any State, in time of peace, except such number only as, in the judgment of the United States, in Congress assembled, shall be deemed requisite to garrison the forts necessary for the defence of such State; but every State shall always keep up a well regulated and disciplined militia, sufficiently armed and accoutred, and shall provide, and constantly have ready for use, in public stores, a due number of field pieces and tents, and a proper quantity of of arms, ammunition and camp equipage.

No State shall engage in any war without the consent of the United States, in Congress assembled, unless such State be actually invaded by enemies, or shall have received certain advice of a resolution being formed by some nation of Indians to invade such State, and the danger is so imminent as not to admit of a delay till the United States, in Congress assembled, can be consulted; nor shall any State grant commissions to any ships or vessels of war, nor letters of marque or reprisal, except it be after a declaration of war by the United States, in Congress assembled, and then only against the kingdom or state, and the subjects thereof, against which war has been so declared, and under such regulations as shall be established by the United States, in Congress assembled, unless such State be infested by pirates, in which case vessels of war may be fitted out for that occasion, and kept so long as the danger shall continue, or until the United States, in Congress assembled, shall determine otherwise.

ART. 7. When land forces are raised by any State for the common defence, all officers of or under the rank of colonel, shall be appointed by the legislature of each State respectively, by whom such forces shall be raised, or in such manner as such State shall direct; and all vacancies shall be filled up by the State which first made the appointment.

ART. 8. All charges of war and all other expences, that shall be incurred for the common defence or general welfare, and allowed by the United States, in Congress assembled, shall be defrayed out of a common treasury, which shall be supplied by the several states, in proportion to the value of all land within each State, granted to or surveyed for any person, as such land and the buildings and improvements thereon shall be estimated according to such mode as the United States, in Congress assembled, shall, from time to time, direct and appoint.

The taxes for paying that proportion shall be laid and levied by the authority and direction of the legislatures of the several states, within the time agreed upon by the United States, in Congress assembled.

ART. 9. The United States, in Congress assembled, shall have the sole and exclusive right and power of determining on peace and war, except in the cases mentioned in the 6th article; of sending and receiving ambassadors; entering into treaties and alliances, provided that no treaty of commerce shall be made, whereby the legislative power of the respective states shall be restrained from imposing such imposts and duties on foreigners as their own people are subjected to, or from prohibiting the exportation or importation of any species of goods or commodities whatsoever; of establishing rules for deciding, in all cases, what captures on land or water shall be legal, and in what manner prizes taken by land or naval forces in the service of the United States, shall be divided or appropriated; of granting letters of marque and reprisal in times of peace; appointing courts for the trial of piracies and felonies committed on the high seas, and establishing courts for receiving and determining, finally, appeals in all cases of captures; provided, that no member of Congress shall be appointed a judge of any of the said courts.

The United States, in Congress assembled, shall also be the last resort on appeal in all disputes and differences now subsisting, or that hereafter may arise between two or more states concerning boundary, jurisdiction or any other cause whatever; which authority shall always be exercised in the manner following: whenever the legislative or executive authority, or lawful agent of any State, in controversy with another, shall present a petition to Congress, stating the matter in question, and praying for a hearing, notice thereof shall be given, by order of Congress, to the legislative or executive authority of the other State in controversy, and a day assigned for the appearance of the parties by their lawful agents, who shall then be directed to appoint, by joint consent, commissioners or judges to constitute a court for hearing and determining the matter in question; but, if they cannot agree, Congress shall name three persons out of each of the United States, and from the list of such persons each party shall alternately strike out one, the petitioners beginning, until the number shall be reduced to thirteen; and from that number not less than seven, nor more than nine names, as Congress shall direct, shall, in the presence of Congress, be drawn out by lot; and the persons whose names shall be so drawn, or any five of them, shall be commissioners or judges to hear and finally determine the controversy, so always as a major part of the judges who shall hear the cause shall agree in the determination; and if either party shall neglect to attend at the day appointed, without shewing reasons which Congress shall judge sufficient, or, being present, shall refuse to strike, the Congress shall proceed to nominate three persons out of each State, and the secretary of Congress shall strike in behalf of such party absent or refusing; and the judgment and sentence of the court to be appointed, in the manner before prescribed, shall be final and conclusive; and if any of the parties shall refuse to submit to the authority of such court, or to appear or defend their claim or cause, the court shall nevertheless proceed to pronounce sentence or judgment, which shall, in like manner, be final and decisive, the judgment or sentence and other proceedings being, in either case, transmitted to Congress, and lodged among the acts of Congress for the security of the parties concerned: provided, that every commissioner, before he sits in judgment, shall take an oath, to be administered by one of the judges of the supreme or superior court of the State where the cause shall be tried, "well and truly to hear and determine the matter in question, according to the best of his judgment, without favour, affection, or hope of reward:" provided, also, that no State shall be deprived of territory for the benefit of the United States.

All controversies concerning the private right of soil, claimed under different grants of two or more states, whose jurisdictions, as they may respect such lands and the states which passed such grants, are adjusted, the said grants, or either of them, being at the same time claimed to have originated antecedent to such settlement of jurisdiction, shall, on the petition of either party to the Congress of the United States, be finally determined, as near as may be, in the same manner as is before prescribed for deciding disputes respecting territorial jurisdiction between different states.

The United States, in Congress assembled, shall also have the sole and exclusive right and power of regulating the alloy and value of coin struck by their own authority, or by that of the respective states; fixing the standards of weights and measures throughout the United States; regulating the trade and managing all affairs with the Indians not members of any of the states; provided that the legislative right of any State within its own limits be not infringed or violated; establishing and regulating post offices from one State to another throughout all the United States, and exacting such postage on the papers passing through the same as may be requisite to defray the expences of the said office; appointing all officers of the land forces in the service of the United States, excepting regimental officers; appointing all the officers of the naval forces, and commissioning all officers whatever in the service of the United States; making rules for the government and regulation of the said land and naval forces, and directing their operations.

The United States, in Congress assembled, shall have authority to appoint a committee to sit in the recess of Congress, to be denominated "a Committee of the States," and to consist of one delegate from each State, and to appoint such other committees and civil officers as may be necessary for managing the general affairs of the United States, under their direction; to appoint one of their number to preside; provided that no person be allowed to serve in the office of president more than one year in any term of three years; to ascertain the necessary sums of money to be raised for the service of the United States, and to appropriate and apply the same for defraying the public expences; to borrow money or emit bills on the credit of the United States, transmitting, every half year, to the respective states, an account of the sums of money so borrowed or emitted; to build and equip a navy; to agree upon the number of land forces, and to make requisitions from each State for its quota, in proportion to the number of white inhabitants in such State; which requisitions shall be binding; and, thereupon, the legislature of each State shall appoint the regimental officers, raise the men, and cloathe, arm, and equip them in a soldier-like manner, at the expence of the United States; and the officers and men so cloathed, armed, and equipped, shall march to the place appointed and within the time agreed on by the United States, in Congress assembled; but if the United States, in Congress assembled, shall, on consideration of circumstances, judge proper that any State should not raise men, or should raise a smaller number than its quota, and that any other State should raise a greater number of men than the quota thereof, such extra number shall be raised, officered, cloathed, armed, and equipped in the same manner as the quota of such State, unless the legislature of such State shall judge that such extra number cannot be safely spared out of the same, in which case they shall raise, officer, cloathe, arm, and equip as many of such extra number as they judge can be safely spared. And the officers and men so cloathed, armed, and equipped, shall march to the place appointed and within the time agreed on by the United States, in Congress assembled.

The United States, in Congress assembled, shall never engage in a war, nor grant letters of marque and reprisal in time of peace, nor enter into any treaties or alliances, nor coin money, nor regulate the value thereof, nor ascertain the sums and expences necessary for the defence and welfare of the United States, or any of them: nor emit bills, nor borrow money on the credit of the United States, nor appropriate money, nor agree upon the number of vessels of war to be built or purchased, or the number of land or sea forces

209

to be raised, nor appoint a commander in chief of the army or navy, unless nine states assent to the same; nor shall a question on any other point, except for adjourning from day to day, be determined, unless by the votes of a majority of the United States, in Congress assembled.

The Congress of the United States shall have power to adjourn to any time within the year, and to any place within the United States, so that no period of adjournment be for a longer duration than the space of six months, and shall publish the journal of their proceedings monthly, except such parts thereof, relating to treaties, alliances or military operations, as, in their judgment, require secrecy; and the yeas and nays of the delegates of each State on any question shall be entered on the journal, when it is desired by any delegate; and the delegates of a State, or any of them, at his, or their request, shall be furnished with a transcript of the said journal, except such parts as are above excepted, to lay before the legislatures of the several states.

ART. 10. The committee of the states, or any nine of them, shall be authorized to execute, in the recess of Congress, such of the powers of Congress as the United States, in Congress assembled, by the consent of nine states, shall, from time to time, think expedient to vest them with; provided, that no power be delegated to the said committee, for the exercise of which, by the articles of confederation, the voice of nine states, in the Congress of the United States assembled, is requisite.

ART. 11. Canada acceding to this confederation, and joining in the measures of the United States, shall be admitted into and entitled to all the advantages of this union; but no other colony shall be admitted into the same, unless such admission be agreed to by nine states.

ART. 12. All bills of credit emitted, monies borrowed and debts contracted by, or under the authority of Congress before the assembling of the United States, in pursuance of the present confederation, shall be deemed and considered as a charge against the United States, for payment and satisfaction whereof the said United States and the public faith are hereby solemnly pledged.

ART. 13. Every state shall abide by the determinations of the United States, in Congress assembled, on all questions which, by this confederation, are submitted to them. And the articles of this confederation shall be inviolably observed by every State, and the union shall be perpetual; nor shall any alteration at any time hereafter be made in any of them, unless such alteration be agreed to in a Congress of the United States, and be afterwards confirmed by the legislatures of every State.

These articles shall be proposed to the legislatures of all the United States, to be considered, and if approved of by them, they are advised to authorize their delegates to ratify the same in the Congress of the United States; which being done, the same shall become conclusive.

# A Note on Sources

This essay is grounded in more than twenty-five years of sustained research into the history of the United States. It thus draws upon the manuscript and other records of the Congress and many divisions of the Executive Department of the federal government, the similar archives of various state governments, numerous personal manuscript collections (and published sets of such correspondence), countless newspaper and magazine articles, and the published and unpublished work of many scholars. The bibliographies and footnotes contained in my earlier books and articles provide a detailed list of such sources.

In preparing this work, however, I did go back to many of those documents, and extended my research into the southern secessionist movement and the reaction of northerners, Abraham Lincoln, and the response to various nineteenth century revolutions.

Beyond the books and articles cited in the footnotes, the following items proved particularly helpful. Not all of them are historical studies. So be it: I am grateful for help from anyone who is committed to community.

Yehoshua Arieli, *Individualism and Nationalism in American Ideology.* Baltimore, Penguin Books, Inc., 1966.

W. H. Auden, "The Fall of Rome," in *Nones*. New York, Random House, 1951.

Shlomo Avineri, *The Social and Political Thought of Karl Marx*. New York, Cambridge University Press, 1968.

Charles and Mary Beard, *The American Spirit*. New York, The Macmillan Company, 1942.

Vance Bourjaily, *The Hound of Earth*. New York, Charles Scribner's Sons, 1955.

Edwin Arthur Burtt, *The Metaphysical Foundations of Modern Physical Science*. New York, Revised Edition, Humanities Press, 1951.

Ernest Callenbach, *Ecotopia*, Berkeley, Calif., Banyan Tree Books, 1975.

G. D. H. Cole, *What Marx Really Meant*. New York, Ryerson Press, 1934.

Robert Coles, *Children of Crisis*. Boston, Atlantic Monthly Press, 1966.

Joseph Conrad, *Nostromo*. Baltimore, Penguin Books, Inc., n.d.

Harold Cruse. *The Crisis of the Negro Intellectual*. New York, William Morrow and Co., 1967.

Moses I. Finley, *Democracy Ancient and Modern*. New Brunswick, Rutgers University Press, 1974.

————, *The Use and Abuse of History*. New York, Viking Press, 1975.

F. Fraser Darling and John P. Milton (Eds.), *Future Environments of North America*. Garden City, N.Y., Natural History Press, 1966.

Eric Foner, *Free Soil, Free Labor, Free Men. The Ideology of the Republican Party Before the Civil War*. New York, Oxford University Press, 1970.

Anatole France, *Penguin Island*. New York, Blue Ribbon Books, 1933.

Romain Gary, *The Roots of Heaven.* New York, Simon & Schuster, 1958.

Paul Goodman, *Growing Up Absurd.* New York, Random House, 1960.

Sebastian de Grazia, *Of Time, Work and Leisure.* New York, Twentieth Century Fund, 1962.

David Green, *The Containment of Latin America.* Chicago, Quadrangle Books, Inc., 1971.

John Howard Griffin, *The Devil Rides Outside.* New York, Pocket Books, Inc., 1952.

Selma von Haden, *Is Cyberculture Inevitable? A Minority View. Fellowship* (January, 1966).

Max Horkheimer, *Eclipse of Reason.* New York, Oxford University Press, 1947.

Merrill Jensen, *The New Nation.* New York, Alfred A. Knopf, Inc., 1950.

K. William Kapp, *The Social Costs of Private Enterprise.* New York, Schocken Books, Inc., 1971.

Weldon Kees, *The Fall of the Magicians.* New York, Reynal & Co., 1947.

Peter Kropotkin, *Fields, Factories, and Workshops; or Industry Combined with Agriculture and Brain Work and Manual Work.* New York, B. Blom, 1968.

Norman Mailer, *The Armies of the Night.* New York, World Publishing Co., 1968.

Bernard Malamud, *The Natural.* New York, Harcourt, Brace and Company, 1952.

Abraham H. Maslow, *Toward A Psychology of Being.* New York, D. Van Nostrand Co., 1962.

F. O. Matthiessen, *American Renaissance.* New York, Oxford University Press, 1941.

Rollo May, *Love and Will.* New York, W. W. Norton & Company, Inc., 1969.

C. B. MacPherson, *The Political Theory of Possessive Indi-*

*vidualism: Hobbes to Locke.* New York, Oxford University Press, 1962.

Klaus Mehnert, *China Returns.* New York, E. P. Dutton & Co., Inc., 1972.

Perry Miller, *Jonathan Edwards.* New York, Meridian Books, Inc., 1959.

Wright Morris, *The Huge Season.* New York, Viking Press, 1954.

———, *The Territory Ahead.* New York, Harcourt, Brace and Company, 1958.

———, *Ceremony in Lone Tree.* New York, Atheneum Publishers, 1960.

Lewis Mumford, *The Pentagon of Power.* New York, Harcourt Brace Jovanovich, Inc., 1970.

Iris Murdock, *Under the Net.* New York, Viking Press, 1954.

———, *The Bell.* New York, Viking Press, 1958.

Bertell Ollman, *Alienation. Marx's Conception of Man in Capitalist Society.* New York, Cambridge University Press, 1971.

Thomas G. Paterson, *Soviet-American Confrontation.* Baltimore, The Johns Hopkins Press, 1973.

Thomas Pynchon, *V, A Novel.* New York, J. B. Lippincott Co., 1963.

Catherine Roberts, *The Scientific Conscience.* George Braziller, Inc., 1967.

E. F. Schumacher, *Small Is Beautiful. Economics As If People Mattered.* New York, Torchbooks, 1973.

———, "The Difference Between Unity and Uniformity," *The CoEvolution Quarterly,* 7 (Fall, 1975), pp. 52-59.

Joseph A. Schumpeter, *History of Economic Analysis.* New York, Oxford University Press, 1954.

Martin J. Sherwin, *A World Destroyed. The Atomic Bomb and the Grand Alliance.* New York, Alfred A. Knopf, 1975.

Adam Smith, *An Inquiry Into the Nature and Causes of The Wealth of Nations*. New York, Modern Library, Inc., 1937.

Henry Nash Smith, *Virgin Land. The American West as Symbol and Myth*. New York, Vintage Books, 1957.

George R. Stewart, *Not So Rich As You Think*. Boston, Houghton Mifflin Co., 1968.

T. S. Stribling, *The Store*. New York, Doubleday, 1932.

Harvey Swados, *On The Line*. Boston, Little, Brown and Co., 1957.

Studs Terkel, *Working*. New York, Bantam Books, 1974.

Thucydides, *The Complete Writings of the Peloponnesian Wars*. New York, Macmillan Company, 1934.

Gore Vidal, *Burr. A Novel*. New York, Random House, Inc., 1973.

Daniel Walden (Ed.), *American Reform: The Ambigious Legacy*. Yellow Springs, Ohio, 1967.

Morris West, *The Devil's Advocate*. New York, Dell Publishing Company, 1967.

Robert H. Wiebe, *The Search for Order, 1877–1920*. New York, Hill & Wang, 1967.

Raymond Williams, *Culture and Society, 1780-1950*. Garden City, N.Y., Anchor Books, 1960.

William Carlos Williams, *In the American Grain*. Norfolk, Connecticut, New Directions, 1925.

R. Jackson Wilson, *In Quest of Community*. New York, John Wiley & Sons, Inc., 1968.

Sheldon S. Wolin, *Politics and Vision. Continuity and Innovation in Western Political Thought*. Boston, Little, Brown and Co., 1960.

# Index

*America Confronts a Revolutionary World*

Everett, Edward, 68
Expansionism
  Adams on, 64, 75-77, 97
  capitalism and, 144
  commerce and, 123-124, 130-132
  freedom and, 101-102
  Hoover on, 162
  isolation and, 92-93
  Jackson on, 95
  Japan, 167-168
  Lincoln on, 114-122
  Madison on, 73, 76, 113, 183-184
  Roosevelt on, 140-142
  self-determination and, 167-168
  Seward on, 122, 125-126
  Texas, 93, 95-97
  U.S.S.R., 175
  Washington on, 77
  Wilson on, 141, 144
Exports, 125, 130-131
  self-determination and, 95

Family, the, 27-29
Fascism, 160, 165, 166
  religion and, 165
Ferdinand VII, King, 66
Feudalism, 47, 165
Finley, Moses I., 181
First Americans, 24, 37, 40, 55, 72, 79-82, 137, 150, 155
  Adams and, 82
  capitalism, 79-81
  counterrevolution, 80
  Jackson and, 82
  Madison and, 81
  Monroe and, 82
  policy of displacement and killing, 80-82, 126
  self-determination, 80, 82, 124, 126
Fish, Hamilton, 128-129
Fiske, John, 123
Foote, Henry Stuart, 92, 104
Ford, Gerald, 179
Forrestal, James V., 175
Four Freedoms, 168
Fourteen Points, 149, 168
France, 35-37, 40, 46, 94-95, 130
  conquest of Mexico, 127-128
  feudalism, 47
  invasion of Spain, 66
  U.S.S.R. and, 166
  World War II, 168
Freedom, 16-17, 32, 36, 40, 43, 49
  commerce and, 132

expansionism and, 101-102
self-determination and, 199
French Revolution, 18-19, 45-58, 64, 129
  isolation and, 60
  Jefferson on, 52-54
  long-term benefits of, 54
  Madison on, 53
  Washington on, 48, 50-51
French West Indies, 55, 95
Freud, Sigmund, 185
Fur trade, 80-81

Gallatin, Albert, 55, 56, 58, 77
Gandhi, Mohandas K., 174, 190
Garrison, William Lloyd, 83, 86
*Gazette of the United States*, 48
Genêt, Edmond Charles, 50-51
Germany, 131, 166, 168, 171
  South America and, 167
  U.S.S.R. and, 166
  World War I, 148-149, 155-156
  World War II, 167
Gilman, Charlotte, 127
Gordon, Thomas, 27
Grant, Ulysses S., 128, 129
Great Britain, 16, 27-29, 39, 40, 50-51, 130, 131
  China and, 134
  Hungary and, 102
  India and, 173-174
  U.S.S.R. and, 166
  War of 1812, 61-62, 73-75
  World War II, 168
Great Depression, 163, 168
Greece, 68-69, 173
  Turkey and, 68
Greeley, Horace, 100, 118

Haiti, 56-57, 147, 162
Haldeman, Richard Jacobs, 129
Hale, John Parker, 102
Hamilton, Alexander, 50
Hamilton, James, 84, 87
Hawaii, 131-132, 155
  self-determination, 131-132
Hayne, Robert Y., 84-86
Higginson, Colonel Stephen, 44, 47
Hilliard, Henry Washington, 99
Hitler, Adolf, 166
Holy Alliance, 66, 67, 69
Hoover, Herbert, 21-22, 154, 158-164, 179-180
  on capitalism, 159-160, 162
  on commerce, 162

**219**

Hoover, Herbert (*cont.*)
  on expansionism, 162
  on individualism, 159
  on self-determination, 160, 161,
    163
  on South America, 162
  Truman and, 179
  Wilson and, 160
Houston, Sam, 96, 97
Hung Siutshuen, 134
Hungary, 100-104, 152
  commerce, 100
  Great Britain and, 102
Hunter, Robert M. T., 102-103
Hunter, William, 103

Imperialism, 20, 38, 42-47, 55-58,
  127, 130-132, 155
*Independent Chronicle*, 54
India, 40, 184, 190
  Great Britain and, 173-174
  self-determination, 173
Indians (American), *see* First
  Americans
Individualism, 127, 182-183
  capitalism and, 124, 150-151, 159
  the community and, 192
  Emerson on, 115
  Hoover on, 159
Ireland, 36
Isolation, 38-46, 73, 109-110
  expansionism and, 92-93
  French Revolution and, 60
  South America and, 60
Israel, 174
  self-determination, 173
  U.S.S.R. and, 175-176
Italy, 166, 178

Jackson, Andrew, 10, 31, 36, 40, 84,
  87, 93, 96
  on commerce, 95
  on expansionism, 95
  First Americans and, 82
  on self-determination, 86
Japan, 134, 135
  China and, 136, 146-147, 162-163,
    166
  expansionism, 167-168
  Wilson and, 146-147, 152
  World War II, 167, 169
Jay, John, 50-51
Jefferson, Thomas, 25, 29, 36-38, 45,
  50, 170, 175, 179, 182
  on commerce, 63

  on the French Revolution, 52-54
  on liberty, 48
  on Montesquieu, 33, 39
  religion, 34
  on self-determination, 74
  on slavery, 77-78
  on uniqueness, 108
Jesus Christ, 185, 189

Kennan, George Frost, 175-177
Kennedy, John F., 23, 42, 109
*Kentucky Gazette*, 45, 48-49
King, Rufus, 73
Kissinger, Henry, 180
Korea, 135, 146, 177-178
  self-determination, 178
Kosciuszko, Tadeusz, 94
Kossuth, Louis, 101-103

La Follette, Robert M., 155-156,
  160-161
League of Nations, 152, 156
Leclerc, Victor, 55
Lee, Arthur, 36
Lenin, Nikolai, 189-190
Leopold III, King, 130
Lewis and Clark expedition, 74
*Liberator*, 83, 86
Liberty, 30-31, 64, 99, 196
  Jefferson on, 48
  power and, 65
  Wilson on, 148
Lieber, Francis, 107
Liliuokalani, Queen, 132
Lincoln, Abraham, 10, 29, 31, 33,
  70-71, 89-92, 96, 105-108, 111-
  122, 170, 174, 177, 184
  arrogance of, 111
  on Blacks, 112
  Calhoun and, 89-90, 108
  on counterrevolution, 112, 119,
    121
  on expansionism, 114, 119-122
  on mission, 121
  on self-determination, 91, 108,
    111-112, 132-133, 183
  on slavery, 89-91, 111-114, 119,
    175
Link, Arthur K., 146
Lippmann, Walter, 179
Livingstone, David, 130
Lloyd, Henry Demarest, 120, 125-
  126
Locke, John, 27
London *Times*, 106, 119